MW00636140

Piecing Together
The
High School
Puzzle

Joanne Mastronicola

The information in this book is provided in good faith for educational and information purposes.

You have permission to use the forms in the back of this book for your own families' use. Please do not duplicate copies of this book or post it on a website. Thank you.

www.highschoolpuzzle.com

ISBN-13 978-0-9844590-0-1
ISBN-10 0-9844590-0-6

Distributed by R.O.C.K. Solid, Inc.
www.rocksolidinc.com
904-751-3569

Okay, mom – the book is done. Thanks to my mom who asked me in nearly every phone conversation we've had in the past two years:

"And ... how's your book coming??"

•••

Through the course of our homeschooling, God has allowed me to glean a lot of information and I want to share it with others – thus this book.

Thanks to both my mom and dad, Joe and Beverly Douthitt, who kept encouraging me to write. Thanks to my sister, Lindley Rachal and our friend, Brenda Boydston who took the time to read through my work and give me excellent pointers.

And lastly, my apologies to our friend, Yvonne Dale, who says ...she desperately needed this years ago.

TABLE OF CONTENTS

CHAPTER 1 – INTRODUCTION

Why I Am Writing This

High School – the time in your life when your children can suddenly reach the stuff on the high shelf for you – the time in your life when their school work begins to scare you a little – the time in your life when you feel like school work suddenly "counts". And … you are deathly afraid of messing it all up and ruining your child's life forever. Well, it may *seem* scary, but it's really not – if you break down the pieces.

You can chart whatever course you desire for your homeschooling student, but whatever you do, ***keep in mind the goal*** so that you are taking the proper steps to get there. Are you heading for ministry, college, or perhaps a particular vocation?

Many parents choose to follow the "traditional" high school path as they feel it makes the transition into college life smoother. They also feel validated by having followed an established course of study. Bear in mind that if your student is college-bound, they will be competing with many students who have followed the "traditional" route. It would be to your student's advantage to meet or exceed these requirements.

This book is written with the intention of giving you the "pieces". When our family began our high school journey, I did all the research myself. I was scared to death that I wouldn't get it all right and it would cause problems for my daughter. I'm not sure why I felt I had to do all this work. Many, many homeschooling parents had gone before me. But, here I was – reinventing the wheel.

We homeschooled our children for 18 years and have just recently graduated our last. My oldest daughter has since obtained her Master's degree from a Florida university. She earned her bachelor's debt-free with the benefit of three scholarships. My second daughter received cosmetology training at a vocational school and because she also earned an academic scholarship, she completed a degree in Art History. Our son worked on a Business Management Technical Certificate at the local state college and wants to eventually start his own business. Can you tell that God gave me three very different children? I have learned a lot and it's not as scary as it once seemed. In fact, I am very confident with what we have done. It's amazing how "educated" you become once you are thrust into a new arena. And, with that "education" comes confidence.

So – I have compiled all of this information for those parents who are coming behind me in an effort to make your path a little easier.

Homeschool vs. Non-Traditional Private School

This book is written specifically for students schooling in the state of Florida, but you can carry a great deal of this information to other states.

In the state of Florida homeschoolers have the option of registering with their local school superintendent and schooling under the homeschool law or schooling under a non-traditional private school, sometimes called an umbrella school.

Under the homeschool law (s. 1002.41), there are three general requirements (1) keep a log, (2) maintain a portfolio, and (3) have your student evaluated. The state of Florida will not issue your student a diploma and you will be responsible for compiling your student's transcript. This book will help you in this area.

Non-traditional private schools establish their own requirements. And many will provide you with a transcript and a diploma upon graduation. In my experience, many such schools also follow the Florida state graduation requirements, perhaps with a few additional requirements of their own.

Throughout this book I will mention both the homeschool law and non-traditional private schools. Keep in mind that they are two *different* avenues, and one may not necessarily mimic the other in its requirements.

A Few Notes:

Please know that I have done my best to be sure all internet addresses listed in this book are current. If you find that the web pages are no longer there, you can most probably do a search and find the needed information.

In addition, the Florida legislature has the ability to modify courses, graduation requirements, university admission requirements, etc., so be sure to verify the presented information – especially if you are several years past this writing.

CHAPTER 2 – OVERVIEW OF LOG, PORTFOLIO, AND EVALUATION

These three items are <u>required</u> under the Florida homeschool law, but you may also be asked to provide these in some form if you are schooling through a non-traditional private school.

Log

The homeschool law requires that you maintain *a log of educational activities that is made contemporaneously with the instruction and that designates by title any reading materials used.*[1] Very simply put – "Write down what you are doing as you do it."

> Write down what you are doing as you do it.

You can keep a log in several different ways. You may purchase a teacher planning book and fill in the squares on a daily basis; writing down the work completed for each subject. You may keep the same information on a large calendar, or you may simply journal your days' work. Many high school students keep their own logs – just be sure to take a look at it from time to time to be sure it is being maintained accurately and completely.

And – it is important that all your records are DATED.

Keeping a log is actually a good way to help students organize their work week. Sit down at the beginning of each week and plan all the week's activities. Be sure to include sports, lessons, church activities, etc. and then schedule out the academics that must also be accomplished during the week. As work gets completed, this can become your log book.

Portfolio

A portfolio is a snapshot of the work you have done to validate your high school credits. It is *samples of any writings, worksheets, workbooks or creative materials used or developed by the student. In addition, the portfolio shall be preserved by the parent for 2 years and shall be made available for inspection by the district school superintendent, or the district school superintendent's agent, upon 15 days' written notice.*[1]

Chapter 5 of this book is devoted to the preparation of a high school portfolio.

Evaluation

An evaluation is a year-end check on your student's progress. The state of Florida requires that *the parent shall provide for an annual educational evaluation in which is documented the student's demonstration of educational progress at a level commensurate with her or his ability. The parent shall select the method of evaluation and shall file a copy of the evaluation annually with the district school superintendent's office in the county in which the student resides. The annual educational evaluation shall consist of one of the following:*

1. *A teacher selected by the parent shall evaluate the student's educational progress upon review of the portfolio and discussion with the student. Such teacher shall hold a valid regular Florida certificate to teach academic subjects at the elementary or secondary level;*
2. *The student shall take any nationally normed student achievement test administered by a certified teacher;*
3. *The student shall take a state student assessment test used by the school district and administered by a certified teacher, at a location and under testing conditions approved by the school district;*

4. The student shall be evaluated by an individual holding a valid, active license pursuant to the provisions of s.490.003(7) or (8) or

5. The student shall be evaluated with any other valid measurement tool as mutually agreed upon by the district school superintendent of the district in which the student resides and the student's parent.[1]

Note that if the student *does not demonstrate educational progress at a level commensurate with her or his ability, the district school superintendent shall notify the parent, in writing, that such progress has not been achieved. The parent shall have 1 year from the date of receipt of the written notification to provide remedial instruction to the student.*[1]

Chapter 7 of this book is devoted to evaluations and testing.

[1]*Quotes are from Chapter 1002 of the Florida Statutes and pertain to students' homeschooling under the homeschool law. You can find this information by going to www.leg.state.fl.us/ and following the link to Florida Statutes.*

CHAPTER 3 – FLORIDA GRADUATION REQUIREMENTS

<u>Overview</u>

In the state of Florida public high school students have several options for obtaining a diploma, including:

1) A four-year, 24 credit program
2) An International Baccalaureate (IB) curriculum
3) An Advanced International Certificate of Education (AICE) curriculum

In order to obtain the IB or AICE credits, teachers and curriculum must be certified by the International Baccalaureate Organization or by the University of Cambridge, respectively. Therefore, if you, as a homeschooler, are interested in pursuing one of these options, you will need to enroll in a school that has gone through this rigorous process.

The 24-credit track includes:

- *4 English Language Arts*
- *4 Mathematics*
- *3 Science (2 with lab components)*
- *3 Social Studies*
- *1 Physical Education*
- *1 Fine or Performing Arts, Speech & Debate or Practical Arts*
- *8 Electives*

College-bound students should meet or exceed the English, math, science and social studies credits and should include two World Language credits in their electives.

In addition to this course requirements, **public school** students are required to take at least one of these courses online and are currently being asked to take End of Course exams for Algebra 1, Geometry, Biology, US History and Algebra 2, if enrolled. These are not legal requirements for homeschooled students.

You can find this public school graduation listing here:

http://www.fldoe.org/core/fileparse.php/7764/urlt/0084250-1415freshmenflyer.pdf

Or go to www.fldoe.org and type Graduation Requirements in the search box. Look for the Academic Advisement flyers.

Notice that I keep pointing out that these are public school requirements and not homeschooling requirements. You do not have to follow these - but we all like checklists — and these are a good standard to follow. Most colleges want to see a minimum of the core work mentioned above.

Feel free to tailor-make your high school graduation requirements for each of your students. Just keep your end goal in mind.

When you plan <u>your</u> high school years — keep in mind the end goal!

Courses	Public School Florida Graduation Requirements 24-credit Standard Diploma
English Language Arts	4 credits (3 with substantial writing for SUS)
Mathematics	4 credits (including Algebra 1 and Geometry)
Science	3 credits (including Biology and 2 equally rigorous courses; 2 courses must include a laboratory component)
Social Studies	1 United States History 1 World History ½ United States Government ½ Economics with Financial Literacy
World Language	Not required for graduation; 2 credits in same language required for college admission/Bright Futures
Fine Arts	1 credit in Fine and Performing Arts, Speech & Debate or specified Practical Arts
Physical Education	1 credit in physical education and health (H.O.P.E.)
Electives	8 credits (at least three strong academic credits if college bound)
Total	24 credits
State Assessment Requirements for **public school** graduation	• Passing scores on the ELA Grade 10 statewide assessment or concordant ACT/SAT score and on the Algebra 1 EOC or a comparative score on the P.E.R.T. • 2.0 GPA on a 4.0 scale • 1 course completed online • Passing scores on End-of-Course (EOC) exams in Algebra 1, Biology 1, Geometry, U.S. History and Algebra 2 if enrolled.

Source: http://www.fldoe.org/core/fileparse.php/7764/urlt/0084250-1415freshmenflyer.pdf

Course Descriptions

Now you know what types of courses your student should be taking – but just what do each of these courses consist of? You can find a description of every high school course in the state system listed at the following website:

http://www.cpalms.org/Public/search/course

This site also provides the course number which can be placed on your transcript. Once you find the course you are interested in, click on the Course Standards box on the right to see a list of expectations for earning this credit. You may want to print out the course description for each course that you are taking to place in your portfolio, although some of them can be quite lengthy.

If you choose to use the state course numbers, review the course description thoroughly to be sure that your coursework lines up with **all** the requirements of the particular course for which you are claiming credit. You do not have to use the state's numbers, but if you do it can make for an easier paperwork transition into Florida colleges.

On the following pages, you will find a breakdown for each subject area....

To find a complete description of all high school courses available in the State of Florida, go to

http://www.cpalms.org/Public/search/course

English Language Arts – 4 credits

English courses **must include major concentration in composition, reading for information and literature**.

Students generally take English 1, English 2, English 3, and English 4, or the Honors or Advanced Placement versions of these four. However, there are many choices and the selection can be a little tricky for some courses.

For those who are college bound, you want to be sure that the courses you are counting towards your English credit are also accepted as such by the college.

To assist you in your labeling, you may want to take advantage of the Comprehensive Course Table (CCT) found here:

https://www.osfaffelp.org/bfiehs/fnbpcm02_CCTMain.aspx

Case in point: Speech (Course #1007300) is found under the Language Arts:Oral Communications section of the Course Descriptions website. When you check the CCT you will see that colleges consider this a course in Performing Fine Arts, not a credit in English Language Arts.

Case #2: Journalism (Course #1006300) is also listed under Language Arts in the Course Descriptions site, but is counted as a Practical Arts Elective by the State University System (SUS)*

*The State University System consists of the eleven public universities in the state of Florida. You will find them listed in the Resources section of this book.

A Quick Look at the Comprehensive Course Table

https://www.osfaffelp.org/bfiehs/fnbpcm02_CCTMain.aspx

The CCT will help you check courses to see if they qualify for regular graduation requirements, (Florida) State University System admission and each level of the Bright Futures Scholarship. Enter the course code number and check the SUS box for a "Y" or "N" to determine how colleges may consider the course.

While you are there, check to be sure one course doesn't negate another. For example – you cannot take both English 2 and English 2 Honors or both English 3 and English Skills 3 as they negate one another. You will find this information listed in each course description as well.

Mathematics – 4 credits

Public school students are required to complete four math courses, one of which should be Algebra 1 and one Geometry. To apply for college all four math courses should be Algebra 1 and higher.

The Algebra 1 graduation requirement may also be met through one of the following options:

- 1200320 Algebra 1 Honors
- 1200370 Algebra 1a **and** 1200380 Algebra 1b
- 1205400 Applied Mathematics 1 **and** 1205410 Applied Mathematics 2
- 1207310 Integrated Mathematics 1 **and** 1207320 Integrated Mathematics 2
- 1200500 Pacesetter Mathematics 1

This can become more than we want to deal with as homeschoolers and there are limitations to counting Algebra 1a and Algebra 1b as two separate credits. As a homeschooler, feel free to take two years to complete a textbook if that's what it takes to master a credit. Just place the credit on your transcript once it has been completed. Many students start Algebra 1 in the 8th grade.

Many universities want you to take at least Algebra 1, Geometry, and Algebra 2 in your high school years. The SAT includes Geometry and Algebra 2 questions and the ACT has a few Trigonometry problems.

> Do not move on if you are not ready. Remember – **mastery** is the key – especially in mathematics courses.

Science – 3 credits...

...two of which must have a laboratory component. This simply means that two of your courses should include hands-on experiments. Most science courses are already set up in this manner.

A traditional course of scientific study includes Biology, Chemistry and Physics. And the public school system wants you to take Biology and two equally rigorous sciences – those typically being Chemistry and Physics. You, of course, may choose other sciences that your student is interested in or continue beyond these three to Anatomy, Zoology, Botany, etc.

Many families have been asking whether Physical Science is still a viable high school credit. Physical Science is still listed in the acceptable list of high school sciences; however, many high schools have removed it from their science track as they want students to take the more rigorous courses listed above.

You may choose among many sciences. Just be sure that you follow the course guidelines, that the description states that it meets the requirements for graduation (or is listed as a core course), and that your student is prepared to meet the demands of whatever course they choose.

By the way – you will note that most sciences include the teaching of evolution. Feel free to teach this from your perspective.

Social Studies – 3 credits:

United States History – 1 credit
World History – 1 credit
United States Government – 0.5 credits
Economics with Financial Literacy – 0.5 credits

There are some really good curriculums out there that cover world history in such great depth that many homeschoolers spend more than one year covering world history – or they get into a very specific time period such as the Civil War. If you like, you can continue with your World Histories for several years and use all of these as your social studies credits. When you look at college application requirements, they are not as specific as the above list – they simply list a requirement of two or three social studies credits.

Another suggestion is to link a literature course to your history studies. For example, the year you study United States History, choose American Literature as your English credit. You will find a couple of curriculums that do this for you already. Example: Notgrass History's *Exploring America* combines American history, American literature and a Bible credit for a total of three high school credits in one text. www.notgrass.com

Whatever you choose to do here, these studies provide great opportunities for you to engage your students in current day political activities in a positive way, so step beyond the books and get involved as you study.

Physical Education – 1 credit

Worded like this: "One credit in physical education to include integration of health." The intention is to group health/life management with physical education into one credit.

Two courses that are currently being used to satisfy this credit are

3026010 – Health Opportunities through Physical Education OR
1506320 – Health Opportunities through Physical Education – Physical Education Variation

That statutes go on to say: "Participation in an interscholastic sport at the junior varsity or varsity level for two full seasons, shall satisfy the one-credit requirement in physical education if the student passes a competency test on personal fitness with a score of "C" or better.....

"Completion of one semester with a grade of "C" or better in a marching band class, in a physical activity class that requires participation in marching band activities as an extracurricular activity, or in a dance class shall satisfy one-half credit in physical education or one-half credit in performing arts....

"Completion of 2 years in a Reserve Officer Training Corps. (R.O.T.C.) class, a significant component of which is drills, shall satisfy the one-credit requirement in physical education and the one-credit requirement in performing arts. This credit may not be used to satisfy the personal fitness requirement or the requirement for adaptive physical education under an individual educational plan (IEP) or 504 plan." (S. 1003.4282)

This means that there are multiple ways to satisfy this requirement if you choose to do so. Note, however, that physical education is NOT listed as a college entrance requirement for the majority of colleges that you may apply for – so don't feel like you have to force this into your curriculum if you aren't already into a physical activity.

Many of our students are actively involved in a sport or physically active hobby and this is a great way to give your student high school credit for something they are already doing.

If your student does want to play sports – especially for a school team, you may wish to contact your local public or private high school and ask about participating in their sports or band programs. It is **important** to note that if you are registered with **a non-traditional private school**, you may need to follow certain guidelines in order to participate with your local public school. Check with the Florida High School Athletic Association at www.fhsaa.org.

And, lastly, if your student aspires to earn an athletic scholarship for college, you should begin looking at the NCAA requirements early. Students must meet certain course requirements and homeschoolers have to keep very detailed records of how they obtained their core credits. www.ncaa.org

Fine Arts – 1 credit

"The practical arts course must incorporate artistic content and techniques of creativity, interpretation, and imagination." (s.1003.4282)

This is usually an easy credit for homeschoolers to meet. We are often involved in dance, music or art on some level. Since we do not typically have a textbook to follow, I would recommend that you copy the course description and take it to any instructor you may be using (or simply review it yourself). If your student is meeting the requirements for the credit to your satisfaction and has completed enough hours of bona fide instruction to equal one credit (135) or a half-credit (67.5 hours) you can feel comfortable including this course on their transcript.

If you have an instructor, you may wish to ask them to write an evaluation of your student's work to include in your portfolio. Pictures are great here too. In order to come up with a fair grade in such a class, I suggest you establish goals at the beginning of the year. If your student achieves a certain level of performance perhaps, or does a certain amount of work, they would earn an "A" – set similar expectations for a B or C grade (remember mastery is the goal – so no Ds or Fs are acceptable.) This will let your student know the expectations and you can feel good about awarding the grade.

World Language – 2 credits

Public school students are not required to take a world language (foreign language) credit in order to graduation; however, many colleges and scholarship applications will require at least two years' credit in the *same* language. American Sign Language does count as a world language.

Although this is rare, you may find that your college will not accept world language credits done at home. Instead they want to see those credits earned through a school – or perhaps validated through testing. This is one of the reasons you will want to start talking with your college-of-choice early on. For those of you considering dual enrolling, these would be great classes to take on the college campus.

Electives – 8 credits

Any course in the 9th – 12th grade course descriptions directory will meet this requirement (except Study Hall ☺).

As noted above, two of these credits should be in foreign language. The balance of your electives can include things like driver's ed, voluntary public service, various sports, research, additional science or math classes, etc. If you are pursuing a specific field in college, your electives should prepare you for that path.

You will find that most college applications expect to see additional academic electives beyond the general core requirements.

STEM

This is a term that you may have seen recently – especially when it comes to high school courses. It is a push for American students to excel in Science, Technology, Engineering and Math. Public school curriculum is being encouraged in this direction and if you have a student who is strong in this area, I expect that we will find more and more challenging homeschooling curriculum available as well.

Really Great News!

Up until the year 2012, the Florida State Statutes specifically stated that any course designated in the Course Code Directory as grade 9 through grade 12 that is taken below the 9th grade may be used to satisfy high school graduation requirements.

This statement disappeared from the 2014 statutes, so at my last visit to a Regional Admissions workshop, I took an informal poll of the college admissions officers there. Everyone that I spoke to said that as long as a high school level course was listed on the transcript, they were willing to consider it for acceptance.

This means that your student may begin high school course work early if they are ready to handle the challenge. For example, many students take Algebra 1 in the 8th grade, to prepare for more rigorous math courses in the 9th through 12th grade years.

Just be sure that you are doing high school level work. For example – do not complete a middle school American History course and give credit for a high school level American History course.

You may find a few colleges that do not want to accept work done outside the 9th-12th grade years, however students who are working ahead of pace typically have plenty of other credits to choose from.

Let's Review

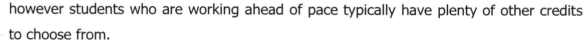

Again, when deciding which course you will take to meet certain requirements, you will want to take advantage of the information in the Comprehensive Course Table.

http://www.osfaffelp.org/bfiehs/fnbpcm02_CCTMain.aspx

It will tell you things like:

- The subject area your course falls under
- The number of credits it can earn
- Whether or not the Florida State University System considers it a core course
- How many high school credits a dual enrolled course earns
- Whether one course negates another. For instance, students who have received a credit in Algebra 1 may not also receive a credit in Algebra 1 Honors, Algebra

1a and 1b, Integrated Mathematics 1 or 2, Applied Mathematics 1 or 2 or Pre-AICE Mathematics 1.

Accelerated Courses

Honors Courses

An honors level course is typically taught at the high school level with a more rigorous component added on. You will find several good descriptions of honors level work in the Florida Course Code Directory (http://www.cpalms.org/Public/search/course).

Most honors courses will typically include a large research project, additional readings and evaluation of those readings or accelerated work above and beyond the typical textbook approach. In other words – more rigorous work – not just additional work.

If you choose to give Honors credit, you may follow the listed guidelines if they are available for the course you are considering. If not, it is recommended that you write a description of the scope of the Honors portion of your course and include proof of that work in your portfolio.

You will find that some of your curricula give an Honors – or more rigorous - option.

I do want to point out that just because a course is more difficult for your student does not automatically make it an honors course. The coursework must go above and beyond the typical high school course.

Advanced Placement® Courses

Advanced Placement courses are taught on a college level. Upon completion of these courses, your student may take the national exam and receive college credit or waiver of equivalent courses in college.

More information is provided in Chapter 4.

International Baccalaureate Courses

The International Baccalaureate Organization offers three programs to schools: The Diploma Programme, the Middle Years Programme and the Primary Year Programme. According to the IBO website (www.ibo.org) "The International Baccalaureate (IB) Diploma Programme is an assessed program for students ages 16 to 19. Through the DP, schools are able to develop students who have excellent breadth and depth of knowledge, flourish physically, intellectually, emotionally and ethically, study at least two languages, excel in traditional academic subjects, and explore the nature of knowledge through the programmes' unique theory of knowledge course."

Homeschoolers do not generally have access to these types of courses without enrolling in an IB World School.

Cambridge Advanced

Also known as AICE (Advanced International Certificate of Education), this is another international, pre-university program and is offered by schools affiliated with the University of Cambridge. Students who complete these courses and pass the required examinations are often offered college credit and higher academic placement in the university system.

As with the IB programme, homeschoolers do not have access to the Cambridge Advanced program unless enrolled in a Cambridge approved school. For more information, go to www.cie.org.uk

Dual Enrollment

Dual Enrollment, sometimes called Concurrent Enrollment or Joint Enrollment, allows your student to take courses at the local state or community college (and some universities) and receive both high school and college credit while still in high school. More detailed information is given in Chapter 4.

It is important to note here that not all dual enrollment courses will meet the Florida State University System _admission_ requirements. You can go to https://www.osfaffelp.org/bfiehs/fnbpcm02_CCTMain.aspx to check a specific course.

Universities will make their own choices about which courses they will accept. If you know to which college you are headed, go ahead and check with their admissions officer.

But – dual enrollment is still an excellent choice, no matter how the course is viewed by the college. It allows your student to slowly enter the college environment. It provides higher level instruction in areas you may be uncomfortable with. Courses are generally free. And odds are good that your student CAN transfer all college credit – especially if they stick with "core" subjects.

To get more information on public school graduation requirements – check here:

http://www.fldoe.org/academics/graduation-requirements/index.stml

Definition of a 'Credit'

Florida state statutes define a credit as follows:

1003.436 Definition of 'credit'.—*(1)(a) For the purposes of requirements for high school graduation, one full credit means a minimum of 135 hours of bona fide instruction in a designated course of study that contains student performance standards.*

You may choose to document a credit in one of two ways. (1) Successful completion of a high school level textbook. (2) Log hours and validate work to complete a specific credit according to the Florida State Course Description.

Do not feel it necessary to keep track of the number of hours you spend with each course. High school level textbooks are written with the idea that a student must spend the required number of hours in order to complete the text. When you are not using a textbook, you may then find it necessary to track hours. See Chapter 6 for a discussion on building a credit when you are not using a traditional textbook.

You may see references stating that <u>150</u> hours equals a full credit (75 hours equals a half credit). Public and private schools often use 54 minute hours (leaving six minutes to change classes) – so in order to get the same number of minutes, they have to get in 150 hours.

Grading Scale

Most schools use the following grading scale for assigning letter grades:

A	90% to 100%
B	80% to 89%
C	70% to 79%
D	60% to 69%
F	0% to 59%

You may wish to hold your student to a higher standard and use the grading scale in which 94% to 100% equals an A. If this is the case, please keep in mind that your student will be competing with other students who will be using the scale above. This could harm a student who earns a 92% - giving them a B while all others receive an A.

Grade Point Average

In order to calculate your student's Grade Point Average (GPA), you assign points to each grade, total the points and divide by the number of credits earned.

You will want to calculate a cumulative GPA only – not a separate one for each year. So, simply total all high school credits and all grade points and find the overall average.

A typical grading scale is the 4.0 scale you will find on the next page. To make the math work, you will see that you need to be sure to cut the GPA in half if the student only earned a half credit for the course. And, to give credit for more rigorous work

> I heard one college admissions officer say "We'll add a full point to your A's, B's and C's, but you worked hard for those D's and F's so we'll let you keep those."

done by the student, you may choose to weight the GPA for Honors, Advanced Placement or dual enrollment courses. You will only want to weight As, Bs and Cs. If a student earned a D in an advanced course, it's a pretty good indication that they did not master the advanced work very well.

When it comes to weighting, some schools give an extra full point to weighted courses, others only give a half point. Whichever you choose, make an indication on your transcript so that those reading the document will know how you calculated your GPA.

I prefer to use the half-point scale because once you submit your transcript to a college, they will assign their own weight scale to your courses and recalculate the GPA. I would much rather have a college bring up my GPA than bring it down because my scale was inflated.

If you have even one course in the mix that is weighted, you now have a weighted GPA. To calculate the unweighted version, you would need to remove the extra points and recalculate. You would then show both a weighted and an unweighted GPA on your transcript.

Weighting means higher point value is given per letter grade because the course content is more academically challenging. This is a way to keep the playing field even when one student takes a heavy academic load while another takes "easy" courses and gets "easy" A's.

Weight Scales for GPA Calculations

Unweighted Quality Points		
Letter Grade	For a **Semester** Course	For an **Annual** Course
A	2.0	4.0
B	1.5	3.0
C	1.0	2.0
D	0.5	1.0
F	0.0	0.0

Half Point Weighted Quality Points		
Letter Grade	For a **Semester** Course	For an **Annual** Course
A	2.25	4.5
B	1.75	3.5
C	1.25	2.5
D	0.5	1.0
F	0.0	0.0

Full Point Weighted Quality Points		
Letter Grade	For a **Semester** Course	For an **Annual** Course
A	2.5	5.0
B	2.0	4.0
C	1.5	3.0
D	0.5	1.0
F	0.0	0.0

Only assign weights to individual courses that can be weighted.

* Bright Futures uses the half-point weighted scale.

Transcripts

A transcript is a list of the courses taken during high school, along with the grade and credit earned. You may wish to include additional information – such as test scores, community service hours, etc. See chapter 6 for various formats and help in building your transcript.

Diplomas

If you are homeschooling under the homeschool law, the local school district will not issue your student a diploma – even if you follow their requirements for graduation. You will issue your own diploma.

If you are homeschooling under a non-traditional private school, you will follow their guidelines for graduation and they will issue a diploma, if they choose.

Questions have been raised about issuing different "types" of diplomas (college-bound, vocational, etc.). Various school systems have designed specific courses of study which will lead to a specific diploma. If you choose to do this, simply place a definition of your diploma type in your portfolio.

No matter what you choose to do about labeling your diploma, I encourage you to evaluate where your child is headed and plan their high school curriculum accordingly. Your transcript will then reflect your specific "track" of education.

You will find a diploma sample in chapter 9.

Let me emphasize once more ....

Rather than focus on what it takes to graduate, you are better served by focusing on what it takes to get where you want to go after graduation.

Universities in the Florida State University System generally have core admission requirements of:

- 4 English (heavy composition and literature)
- 4 Math (Algebra 1 and above)
- 3 Science (2 with labs)
- 3 Social Studies
- 2 World Language (same language)
- Strong academic electives
- Qualifying GPA and college entrance test scores. Generally if one of these is high, the other may be a little lower. A higher test score will allow you to get away with a lower GPA.

You will also want to be sure that your electives work towards your goal.

If you are heading to a college outside the Florida State University System – be sure to check their requirements early on.

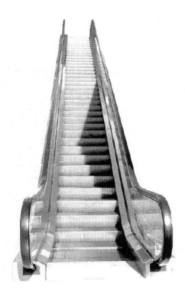

CHAPTER 4 – WAYS TO OBTAIN COURSES

Complete Curriculum Packages

While some publishers specialize in only one high school subject, many publishers provide an entire high school package – including many electives.

By choosing to follow most publishers' entire course, you can guarantee that you "check all the boxes" and expose your student to a well-rounded high school education. Often these publishers will provide additional teacher helps and ways to track all course work completed so that you can compile a transcript upon completion.

Other organizations have assembled entire curriculum packages from various publishers to help you cover all the bases in your high school years. Some well known resources that will help you with the entire package are:

- A Beka Book – www.abeka.com
- Bob Jones University Press – www.bjupress.com
- Calvert School – www.calvertschool.org
- Central Christian Academy – www.acces-inc.com

While many families choose to use one source exclusively, you have the ability to "pick and choose" from various publishers. For example, you may wish to use the foreign language curriculum of one publisher, yet follow the math courses of another. This is perfectly acceptable.

Some specialty area curriculums can be found at:

- Apologia Sciences – www.apologia.com
- Math-U-See – www.mathusee.com
- Notgrass History and Literature – www.notgrass.com
- Institute for Excellence in Writing – www.iew.com

Distance or Online Learning

A distance learning course is one in which work is laid out for your student, typically online, and is graded or evaluated by someone other than the parent. Often distance learning courses will keep records for you and provide documentation for a transcript and a maybe even a diploma upon completion. You may choose to do your entire high school work via this method, or only use it to obtain one or two courses.

The benefits to this type of work are that someone oversees your student's progress and will maintain your records. An independently motivated student will do well with these types of courses.

There are many, many distance learning courses available – simply do an internet search for homeschool distance learning courses and you'll see what I mean (over 43 million hits when I tried it). Be sure to research each carefully – asking to see samples of curriculum and confirming exactly what you get for the fee they charge. You want to be sure that your student will be academically challenged.

Often there are tiered fee schedules – one fee for the course, another for keeping records, etc.

Some well-known distance learning courses are:

- Abeka – www.abekaacademy.org
- Bob Jones – www.bjupress.com and search distance learning
- Central Christian Academy – www.acces-inc.com
- Christian Liberty Academy – www.homeschools.org
- K12 – www.k12.com
- Florida Virtual School – www.flvs.net
- Seton Home Study – www.setonhome.org

Florida Virtual School is a popular choice for homeschoolers. Because online classes are also available to public school students, be sure to follow the homeschool links and register as a homeschooler with FLVS. If not, you will find yourself in the public system with an assigned guidance counselor and required courses. If this has happened to you, simply call FLVS and they can help you re-label yourself in their system.

FLVS has added some very interesting courses over the last few years including Forensic Science, Law Studies, Theater, Cinema and Film Production and Creative Photography.

You may also contact Florida Virtual School by calling 800-374-1430.

Florida Virtual School offers many Honors and AP courses as well as AP Test Review (on their mobile app). Registration is open year-round and classes are generally filled on a first-come, first-served basis (with some exceptions, such as a senior needing a specific course to graduate.) There is currently no fee for Florida residents. All three of my children have taken advantage of these courses and we have found them to be a convenient way to pick up courses each year. You will find the content both complete and challenging.

Computer Programs

Besides online courses, there are many software packages out there that will not only provide instruction to your high school student, but will test them, keep track of grades and generate a transcript upon completion of their work.

Alpha Omega's <u>Switched-on Schoolhouse</u> series is a popular one that I am familiar with. You can complete your entire high school course via this method if you are inclined to do so. I only recommend a student take a full load via computer if they are okay with sitting at a computer for hours on end. I know many students who can do this easily – I also know of many students who would go bananas if they had to face a computer screen for long periods of time.

But – even if you are not willing to use an entire computer package, there are many 'subject-specific' computer courses available and loads of CDs and DVDs to supplement textbook work. Apologia's "Exploring Creation Through…." science courses all have CDs which contain the entire course. Dr. David Shormann has an excellent series of D.I.V.E. (Digital Interactive Video Education) CDs that supplement Saxon Math textbooks. Nearly every publisher has a computerized version of or supplement to their product.

To locate many of these items, check out the sources listed in the Appendix or do an internet search for high school curriculum software.

Tutors

Many parents feel that they cannot possibly teach all the "difficult" high school courses. And, often rightly so – especially if you have more than one high school student.

It is not an admission of weakness to seek outside help. There are many tutors available to help your high school student. Some tutors will advertise their services via your local home school group. These are often school teachers looking for some additional income. Or – you may find a more advanced high school student or even a college student with strengths that can benefit your student.

Sometimes you will need a tutor simply to help you "over a hump" – but often you will need a tutor to get through an entire course. I have found this especially true when you reach the higher level math courses.

If you cannot afford to pay for these services, you may be able to barter for them. We have a wonderful teacher in our area that has chosen to stay home with her young children. Rather than accept payment for her services, she often barters for them. She has received appliance repair, complete carpet cleanings, major yard work, tile work, house cleanings, etc. in exchange for tutoring.

I do recommend that you compensate your tutor in some manner. You will find your tutor more reliable if they are receiving some sort of income.

High School Co-ops and Paid Classes

High school co-ops are popular in many areas of the state. They generally meet one or two days a week, allowing students to take several different courses during the day and then completing their course work at home throughout the week. Parents often teach or facilitate in their area of expertise – taking advantage of each others' skills. Each co-op has its own requirements, so if this avenue interests you, check around to see which co-op fits your needs best. This is an option you should consider early – probably in the spring – as many co-ops have a deadline for enrolling.

You may also wish to locate classes that are available for a fee. Often a tutor or group of tutors will offer small classes in their area(s) of expertise. Your student would attend classes a few times during the week and complete the balance of their work at home. As the homeschooling parent, you are still responsible for overseeing the work and keeping the records – you would just have assistance in teaching the course material.

Advanced Placement® Courses

The Advanced Placement Program® offers academically challenging courses to high school students. These courses are taught at the college level and require that you have completed the necessary prerequisites for the course. Courses receive their AP designation by following the content and curricular goals outlined in the AP Course Description booklets.

Participating colleges offer credit or waiver of equivalent courses for successful completion of a national exam. Students enrolled in Advanced Placement® courses are being prepared to take the exam. You may wish to locate AP courses in your area and talk with the provider about your student taking them. You will find many AP courses as well as AP Test Review available through Florida Virtual School – www.flvs.net.

Students who do not have access to an AP course are still eligible to take the AP exam. You just want to be sure you prepare well for the test. You can find plenty of information on exam preparation at apcentral.collegeboard.com/home. Parents and students are not eligible to order the exams, though, so you must contact your local school with an AP program and make arrangements to take the exam through them. You should contact your local school by February to give them plenty of time to place your order.

As of this writing, AP exams are offered in the following areas:

Arts

Art History

Music Theory

Studio Art: 2-D Design

Studio Art: 3-D Design

Studio Art: Drawing

English

English Language and Composition

English Literature and Composition

History & Social Science

Comparative Government & Politics

European History

Human Geography

Macroeconomics

Microeconomics

Psychology

United States Government & Politics

United States History

World History

STEM

Biology

Calculus AB

Calculus BC

Chemistry

Computer Science A

Environmental Science

Physics 1

Physics 2

Physics C: Electricity and Magnetism

Physics C: Mechanics

Statistics

World Languages & Cultures

Chinese Language and Culture

French Language and Culture

German Language and Culture

Italian Language and Culture

Japanese Language and Culture

Latin

Spanish Language and Culture

Spanish Literature and Culture

AP exams are given on specific dates at the end of the school year. The cost runs about $91 per exam and results are usually received the first of July.

Dual Enrollment

Dual Enrollment, sometimes called Concurrent Enrollment or Joint Enrollment, allows high school students, generally in the 11th and 12th grades, to attend a state or community college and obtain both high school and college credit for courses taken there.

If your student is enrolled in a non-traditional private school, your school must typically have an articulation agreement with the community college. If you are schooling under the homeschool law, courses are available to you as well. Simply contact the dual enrollment counselor at your local college and ask for information. You will want to do this early – often at least a semester ahead of the time you would like to attend.

Each community college will have its own requirements for enrolling, including minimum age, minimum college entrance test scores [ACT, SAT or the P.E.R.T. - Postsecondary Education Readiness Test], minimum GPA and number of college credits your student is allowed to take.

See Chapter 7 for further information on obtaining College Admission testing.

Dual enrollment fees will depend upon whether you are enrolling as a homeschooled student or as a private school student from a non-traditional private school. Some colleges do not charge, or charge only for books and lab fees while others will require that you pay tuition.

NOTE – It is very important that you go through your dual enrollment counselor when registering for classes. Not following their guidelines could result in a loss of credit and a bill for full tuition.

For the most part, a three-hour college course (one semester) will convert to a half credit for high school. However, there are exceptions to this rule. The Articulation Coordinating Committee has given well over 100 college courses one full high school credit for a semester's work. For example: College Algebra, several science courses, all four-credit foreign languages, etc. count as one full high school credit. You can determine how much high school credit is earned by going to www.fldoe.org and searching for the *High School Subject Area Equivalency List*.

... or going to the Comprehensive Course Table found here:

https://www.osfaffelp.org/bfiehs/fnbpcm02_CCTMain.aspx

CHAPTER 5 – YOUR PORTFOLIO

Preparing a Portfolio

You will want to either prepare a separate portfolio for each year or an entire portfolio for your high school years.

A portfolio is a "snapshot" of the work you have done to validate your high school credits. It is NOT every single piece of work you have generated. While that may be impressive because of sheer volume, it is very difficult to digest should anyone want to actually read through it.

While the homeschool law requires that you keep your student's portfolio for at least two years, I highly recommend that you keep their high school portfolio indefinitely. I have a friend whose son was in his third year at a Florida university when he applied for a position in a government academy. Because he had been homeschooled, this academy wanted proof of his high school activity – *even though he had an AA degree and was currently doing very well in college!* While we could all stand and argue the rationale behind that request, sometimes it is just more impressive to present the information in a well-documented form.

Showcase your student's best work and provide "proof" that you have covered the course content.

Many forms can be found in the appendix of this book to aid you in building your portfolio.

You may choose to keep your portfolio in either a three-ring notebook or a hanging file system. There are many excellent storage systems available at office supply stores that will work nicely.

I keep a three-ring notebook for each of my children for each year. I use a 2" viewbinder so that I can label the spine with their name and year. You could even put a picture of them in the front pocket.

I then make dividers <u>for each subject</u> they are taking that year and behind each divider I place the following items:

- Copy of the State of Florida course requirements for that subject *(Found at* http://www.cpalms.org/Courses/CourseDescriptionSearch.aspx*)*. Note that some of these descriptions may be inordinately long, so instead ...
- You could choose to copy the course description from your curriculum publisher's website – they will often give a good overview of their material and how it relates to a high school credit.
- A list of textbooks and curriculum aids used for that course, including software, tutors, etc. You may also want to photocopy the table of contents from your textbook and place it here.
- A list of books read if this course contains literature.
- Samples of work from throughout the year. Collect five or more samples of work for each *quarter* and choose the ones that match the course requirements found at the website listed above.

In addition to a section for each course completed, at the beginning of your notebook, you will want a section for personal information. You will also need sections for test scores, awards and achievements, and jobs held.

So, let's go through each of these sections in detail:

Personal Information

This section is simply an area in which to gather information that may need to be passed on to college or scholarship committees. It should contain the following:

- Student's full name
- Address and contact information
- Other names the student may have used
- Date of birth
- Social security number*
- Immunization record
- Health exam record (especially for athletes)
- Any special needs testing
- Any IQ testing
- List of schools previously attended with addresses

*While many families are reluctant to provide their student's social security number, you may find it necessary to do so in order to qualify for many scholarships and to enroll in college. I just wouldn't put it on any paperwork until it's absolutely necessary. Many colleges now assign a student ID number to make it easy to match paperwork.

Individual Courses

You will want a section for each high school level course you have completed. Here are some items you may wish to include in each section.

- Course descriptions (from either the state course website listed earlier or the curriculum provider).

- A list of textbooks, tutors, computer programs, reading books, etc. used in the completion of this course.
- Samples of work per subject.

Samples of Work Shown

- Should line up with the course requirements
- Should be spread out through the duration of the course (beginning, middle, end),
- Can show a work in progress
- Can be photos or video recordings of work projects

Be sure to DATE all of your samples – *I have discovered that "we homeschoolers" often have a hard time dating work, but it is a good habit to get into and it is necessary.*

Specific subject samples could include:

<u>English</u>
- Photocopies from grammar workbooks
- Original papers or paragraphs written by student (no plagiarism*)
- Critiques of books read
- Research papers – show a work in progress, or include first drafts as well as final products
- Because of the diversity of an English credit – reading, grammar, composition, literature studies, etc. – it would be good to include more samples in this subject than in others.

*Be sure you spend time with your student and explain fully what **plagiarism** is. The Oxford English Dictionary says it means "**to take and use as one's own the thoughts, writings, or inventions or another.**" Learn how to properly cite sources used in your writings.

Math

- Photocopies from math workbooks
- Math papers, ***including work shown***
- Math corrections
- Tests

> Students who organize their math work neatly on their papers – writing out all the steps to the problem – tend to score higher in their work.

Science

- Answers to questions at the back of chapters (include questions, or write your answers in complete sentences)
- Copies from student's lab manuals
- Pictures of lab work being done
- Science research projects
- Papers written
- Tests taken

Social Studies

- Answers to questions at the back of chapters (include the questions or write your answers in complete sentences)
- Papers written
- Tests taken
- Photos of field trips

World Languages

- Vocabulary lists
- Sentences or paragraphs written
- Photocopies out of workbooks
- Written assignments
- Logs of oral assignments, perhaps even videos of speeches

Sports

- Log of time spent at practice and in games
- Photos of student participating in sports
- Research done on the sport
- Paper on safety factors in the sport
- Research on nutrition and sports
- Demonstration of student's knowledge of the rules of the game
- Evaluation of student's skill by coach
- Research on exercise

> Public school students take Health Opportunities through Physical Education (H.O.P.E.) for their basic PE credit. You will find information on this credit in Chapter 3.

Drivers Ed

Course # 1900300
Driver Education/Traffic Safety Classroom

Course #1900310
Driver Education/Traffic Safety Classroom and Lab

Because different insurance companies vary in what they will allow for student discounts, you may want to check with your insurance company prior to beginning this course. If you are enrolled in a non-traditional private school, local public high schools are not "required" to allow your student to attend their Driver's Ed course. However, many are still open and friendly to your student.

National Driver Training Institute offers a Driver's Ed course for which they will issue a certificate upon completion. You may check their website at www.nationaldrivertraining.com. This course is also carried by R.O.C.K. Solid (www.rocksolidinc.com).

1-800-942-2050 – National Driver Training

1-800-705-3452 – R.O.C.K. Solid

And, of course, there are many private local companies who offer driver training to your student for a fee. But, the money you save on your insurance may be well worth the fee. We paid about $200 for our daughter's driver training, but saved $400 per year in insurance. Pretty good economics if you ask me.

World Languages

As mentioned in chapter 3, not all students are required to take a world (foreign) language in order to graduate; however, many colleges and scholarships will require at least two years' credit in the same language. Also note that while most colleges (including all in the Florida State University System) recognize American Sign Language as a foreign language, a *very few* do not. (E-mail your college of choice and ask.)

There are many options for taking world languages including textbooks, co-op courses, online courses, and dual enrollment.

One popular choice is dual enrollment. One semester of world language in a four-hour dual enrollment course equals one high school credit in world language. This means your student can complete his world language requirements in one year. The foreign language lab allows your student to receive one-on-one tutoring in the language of their choice, and there are often many different languages to choose from.

You will find that some state universities require that homeschooled students obtain their world language either through dual enrollment, Florida Virtual School or a private school. Again – a very few – but check with your college of choice early.

Awards and Achievements

It is good to include a list of all your student's awards and achievements in the form of a high school resume. (See sample in the Appendix.) If you're like me, by the time you are being asked for that information in your student's senior year, you've forgotten about all those things accomplished while they were freshmen, so write it down and keep it in one location – no matter how insignificant you feel it may be.

You'll find a form for listing awards and achievements in the Appendix as well.

Jobs Held

Some scholarships ask for an accounting of jobs held while the student attended high school. Keep a general log that includes:

- Starting and ending dates of employment
- Type of work done
- Name and contact information of supervisor
- Approximate number of hours worked weekly
- Approximate number of weeks worked during the year
- Promotions and pay raises earned
- Special recognitions on the job
- Any supervisory work done

Under Child Labor Laws in the state of Florida, students may apply for a waiver to work additional hours, or during regular school hours. You may obtain the necessary forms by visiting:

http://www.myfloridalicense.com/dbpr/reg/childlabor/

Scroll down to see the Child Labor Waiver form. Or you may call the Department of Business and Professional Regulation Bureau of Child Labor at (800) 226-2536.

You may wish to give your student a high school credit in work experience or vocational training. You will find a job evaluation form in the Appendix that may be completed by your child's employer to aid in validating this credit. By going to www.fldoe.org/workforce/dwdframe/ you will find details on many vocational credits available in the state of Florida.

Volunteer School/Community Service

The State of Florida course requirements for "Volunteer School/Community Service" require documentation of 75 hours of community service. This documentation should be in the form of a letter or form from the volunteer organization listing the type of work done, the number of hours served and a signature of someone in the organization attesting to the work.

Credit may not be earned for <u>paid</u> work – nor may it be earned for community service provided as a result of court action.

Also, some scholarships applications do not accept ministry or political work as "community service". The key seems to be whether you are proselytizing for your "cause". Many homeschooled students are active in ministries, just be sure that your student can document volunteer work that would not be considered "converting someone to your way of thinking".

If you do not wish to give a high school credit, but still need to have it documented for scholarship considerations, obtain a signed acknowledgment from the agency or agencies for which the service was done.

There is a sample volunteer letter in the Appendix you may wish to copy or change for your personal use.

Check out this website for scholarships based on volunteer work:

www.finaid.org/otheraid/service.phtml

CHAPTER 6 – BUILDING A TRANSCRIPT and ISSUING A DIPLOMA

A transcript is an outline of all the courses your student has completed during school years, showing the credit and grade earned for each course. It can contain as much or as little information as you like, but the goal is to make it clear, concise and readable.

You will want to include the title of the course, the grade earned and the number of credits earned for each class. If you have followed the course requirements for a class listed in the Florida high school course directory, you may also choose to list that seven-digit number. For dual enrollment courses, you can list the college course number.

You may also wish to include information on how courses were administered, year-end test scores, extracurricular activities, etc. I have seen transcripts range from one to nine pages.

You will find a few sample transcripts in the back of this book. Choose the format that works best for you.

> I recommend a one to two page overview, along with a high school resume giving bullet points outlining your student's achievements during high school.

It is important that you keep your transcript up to date each year. Nothing's worse than getting to the end of the road and discovering that either you have forgotten work that was completed, or you failed to complete the correct requirements for your charted course.

At the end of each year, print a current transcript that includes all high school courses to date and file it in your student's portfolio.

To help you maintain the information that will be placed on your transcript, you may wish to use a Tracking Worksheet. (Sample and blank copies are in the back of this book.)

This Tracking Worksheet is a work in progress, so write in pencil and be willing to change course if necessary. This is an excellent planning tool and will allow you to keep on track. You would hate to get to the end of the road and discover that you missed a math credit.

Keep this *worksheet* in the front of your portfolio to assist you in planning your school years.

It is okay to take longer than one year to earn a single credit. If you are using a transcript form which shows dates, simply put the date completed.

It is also okay to take a longer (or shorter) time to complete your high school work. Some students take five years to obtain their 24 credits while others take only three. Just be certain that the course has been completed <u>entirely</u> and that you have been able to document it well.

If you have a student who is a high achiever and they are able to complete their credits prior to age 16, you may find it a challenge to proceed into the college arena, simply because of age. Having a well-documented portfolio will assist you here. In addition, their college entrance test scores should validate their course work and grades.

You should not accept a grade of 'D' or lower for your students. It shows they have not mastered the material. If they make less than a "C", require them to take the entire course over in order to receive the credit.

Looking at the various formats for transcripts you will note that you can choose to list all the same subjects together, or you can list your subjects by year completed. Just be sure to stay consistent so that your transcript is readable.

Textbook Credits versus Building Your Own

If you are taking a textbook course such as Algebra 2, in which the coursework is done from a traditional text, completion of this textbook should also mean completion of the course requirements. Just check the course requirements to see that you've covered everything.

However, if you are NOT using a textbook, you will often find it necessary to "build" your credit. In these cases, it would be wise to document well the course requirements, the manner in which you met each of these requirements and the time spent doing so.

For example, your student is playing soccer for the local soccer association. Can you give them a credit in soccer (course #1503320)? In addition to actually playing the sport, a few of the requirements for this course are:

- Select and apply sport/activity specific warm-up and cool-down techniques
- Analyze and evaluate the risks, safety procedures, rules, and equipment associated with specific course activities.
- Analyze the role of games, sports and/or physical activities in other cultures.

Obviously, your student will not obtain all of this knowledge by simply playing the sport. You will need to supplement their game with some research. You could also have the coach complete an evaluation of your student's progress or ability. And lastly, you also need to verify that the student has completed at least 67.5 hours of work (remember that 135 hours equals a full credit) – keeping a time log should suffice nicely.

Diploma Types

As I mentioned in chapter three, if you are homeschooling under the homeschool law, the local school district will **not** issue your student a diploma – even if you follow their requirements for graduation. Many just recommend that your student take the GED. *(I do not recommend taking the GED unless your next stage in life specifically requests it.)*

If you are homeschooling under a non-traditional private school, many are willing to issue a diploma to your student provided that you follow their guidelines for graduation.

Questions have been raised about issuing different types of diplomas (college-bound, vocational, etc.) Feel free to label your diploma with a specialty if you'd like. Typically that means that your student has taken a significant amount of courses in a given area. Or, you can choose to issue a standard diploma and let your transcript of work speak for itself.

As a homeschooling parent, you can issue your own diploma and have it signed by the principal of your school. Office supply stores have certificate paper and you can create your diplomas on your computer. See a sample in chapter 9.

For a nice touch, you can even order diploma covers from graduation supply companies. You will find a list at the end of the book.

GED – General Educational Development Test

In order to achieve some of your continuing education goals, you may be required to take the GED. We all know that for some the GED carries a certain stigma with it, however, it still may be a course you wish to pursue. The internet lists Bill Cosby, Michael J. Fox, Peter Jennings, Dave Thomas and Mary Lou Retton among the list of famous people who have taken the GED to complete their high school education.

To obtain information on taking the GED, go to www.gedtestingservice.com or contact your local school district or state college. A new, more challenging version of the test was released in 2014, and it is now given on computer rather than paper. You can find specific test information at www.gedtestingservice.com/educators/2014test.

You are expected to have at least a 9th grade reading level and will be tested on language arts, social studies, science and mathematical reasoning.

There are several preparation books to help you prepare for the GED – two popular sources are <u>Barron's How to Prepare for the GED Test</u> and <u>Kaplan GED Test Strategies, Practice and Review.</u>

> Check out www.4tests.com for free practice tests.

CHAPTER 7 – EVALUATIONS AND TESTING

Year End Testing

If you are schooling under the homeschool law in the state of Florida, you must obtain an annual evaluation of your student.

Under this homeschool law (Florida statute 1002.41), you are given five choices:

1. A teacher selected by the parent shall evaluate the student's educational progress upon review of the portfolio and discussion with the student. Such teacher shall hold a valid regular Florida certificate to teach academic subjects at the elementary or secondary level;

2. The student shall take any nationally normed student achievement test administered by a certified teacher;

3. The student shall take a state student assessment test used by the school district and administered by a certified teacher, at a location and under testing conditions approved by the school district;

4. The student shall be evaluated by an individual holding a valid, active license pursuant to the provisions of s.490.003 (7) or (8).

5. The student shall be evaluated with any other valid measurement tool as mutually agreed upon by the district school superintendent of the district in which the student resides and the student's parent.

In addition, many non-traditional private schools require that your student be evaluated on an annual basis.

There are many avenues available to you for testing and/or evaluations. Contact your local homeschool support group to see what is available in your area. You can find local support groups by contacting the Florida Parent Educators Association (FPEA) at www.fpea.com or toll-free at 1-877-ASK-FPEA.

Or --- you can contact the following agencies who provide testing to homeschooled students:

BJU Home Education Services
1-864-770-1381
www.bjup.com/services/testing/

Christian Liberty Academy
1-800-349-0899
www.shopchristianliberty.com/special-service/

Seton Testing Services
1-800-542-1066
www.setontesting.com
testing@setontestingcom

Just do an online search for 'homeschool achievement testing' and see the many, many testing suppliers that are out there. You'll also find a list on the HSLDA website: www.hslda.org/earlyyears/Testing.asp

Keep in mind that it is your responsibility to obtain testing or evaluation each year and submit the results to the proper authorities in a timely fashion.

As of this writing, Florida homeschooled students are not required to take the public school year-end or End-of-Course assessments in order to graduate. This is a public *school requirement only. You will want to bear this in mind, however, if you plan to return your student to the school system for graduation.*

End of Course (EOC) Exams

The Florida public school system has recently introduced End of Course (EOC) exams for several subjects, including Algebra 1, Geometry, U.S. History and Biology courses. In order to earn the corresponding credit, students must pass these exams. Any student transferring into a public high school without having taken these may be required to take the exam before a diploma is issued. Each principal is given the authority to make this decision.

Tied to the EOC exams is the Credit Acceleration Program (F.S. 1003.4295) which allows public school students to earn high school credit for the course by simply taking the EOC exam and not the class. While this is a possible option, personally I'm not a fan of testing out of such foundational courses – there is power in the journey.

Public school students must also pass the Grade 10 level of the English Language Arts (ELA) exam. <u>None</u> of these exams are required for homeschooling students.

College Admission Testing

College admission test scores are used to determine your student's admission into college. Each college will have its own minimum score requirements. In addition, test scores can be used to determine which classes you are placed in.

Keep in mind that test scores are not the only factor in determining whether you get into college – and you may take tests more than once to improve your scores. So, prepare adequately for the tests, but do not stress unduly over poor results.

PSAT (Preliminary SAT and National Merit Scholarship Qualifying Test)

This test is used to prepare your student for the SAT. The PSAT is administered once a year during the month of October. It is generally taken in the 11th grade (but may be taken in the 9th and 10th grades as well). You may contact a local high school and take the test through them, or, several non-traditional private schools and state colleges throughout the state provide testing centers as well. Go to www.collegeboard.com/psat and look for the "high school search" link to find a school near you that will be administering the PSAT.

You may also contact your local support groups for more information. The fee is generally in the neighborhood of $14.

The PSAT gives the student practice for the actual SAT, but more importantly, 11th grade PSAT scores are used to determine qualification for the National Merit Scholarship. Some parents feel that it is okay to skip this test – and while it is not used for college admission, there is a great deal of scholarship money tied to this score.

The PSAT/NMSQT measures critical reading, mathematics and writing skills. Each section is currently scored 20 to 80 (comparable SAT sections are scored 200 to 800), with average scores falling in the 40s. National Merit Qualifying scores will be in the high 70s. The scoring system will be changing to align with SAT scoring of 200-800.

The redesigned PSAT rolls out in fall of 2015. The new structure will align with the scheduled update to the SAT (rolling out spring 2016). There will also be an PSAT 8/9 version for 8th and 9th graders coming out 2015 and a PSAT 10 launching in February 2016.

Visit www.collegeboard.com/psat for more information.

SAT

This is the test used for college admission. Do not confuse it with the Stanford Achievement Test, often used for year-end evaluations for 1st through 12th graders.

The SAT is offered seven times a year with many testing locations throughout the state. The fee is about $53 and you may register online at www.collegeboard.com.

> When I say "about $53" it is because you have several options for reporting the scores, some of which have an additional fee.

Currently there are three sections to the test – Critical Reading, Math and Writing. Each section will receive a score of 200 to 800; therefore a perfect score is 2400. You will also receive two sub-scores in the writing section: a multiple-choice score from 20 to 80 and an essay score from 2 to 12. In Spring of 2016 a new version of the test will be coming out and will drop the Writing section.

Each of the above sections break down as follows:
- Reading: Sentence completion and Passage-based reading
- Math: Multiple choice and Student-produced responses
- Writing: Improving sentences, Identifying sentence errors, Improving paragraphs and Essay

The Florida Bright Futures Scholarship does not use the Writing section score to determine Bright Futures eligibility. Yet, many colleges do look at this score.

The Florida Bright Futures Scholarship, as well as many colleges, will "mix and match" SAT test scores to obtain a super score. This means that they will take the highest score from each section of the test to come up with your highest possible overall score. For example, if you were to score 600 on Critical Reading and 600 on Math for the SAT – then the next time you take it, you score 700 on Critical Reading, but you drop to 550 on Math – the college will take the two highest – 700 on Critical Reading and 600 on Math, for a total of 1300 for those two sections.

I highly recommend using some sort of SAT preparation before taking the SAT. My daughter took the test in the 10th grade, just for practice, and then in addition to covering more mathematics in her course work, she took an SAT prep course. Her score increased 330 points in just one year.

College Prep Genius (www.collegeprepgenius.com) is an excellent SAT test prep program. You can purchase their materials and do the work at home or take advantage of their many workshops. This is time well spent as it can pay off in scholarship dollars.

SAT Reasoning Test Sections

- Writing Section
  - 25 minute essay and 49 multiple choice questions
  - 25 questions – improving sentences
  - 18 questions – identifying sentence errors
  - 6 questions – improving paragraphs
- Math Section
  - 44 multiple choice and 10 student-produced responses
    - Covering numbers and operations, algebra and functions, geometry and measurement, data analysis, statistics and probability
- Critical Reading Section
  - 48 passage-based reading and 19 sentence completions
    - Covering extended reasoning, literal comprehension and vocabulary in context
- Each section will have a score of 200 to 800.

Taken from www.collegeboard.com – March 2015

Essay Prompt:

Think carefully about the issue presented in the following excerpt and the assignment below.

We are often told to "put on a brace face" or to be strong. To do this, we often have to hide, or at least minimize, whatever fears, flaws, and vulnerabilities we possess. However, such an emphasis on strength is misguided. What truly takes courage is to show our imperfections, not to show our strengths, because it is only when we are able to show vulnerability – or the capacity to be hurt – that we are genuinely able to connect with other people.

Assignment: Is it more courageous to show vulnerability than it is to show strength? Plan and write an essay in which you develop your point of view on this issue. Support your position with reasoning and examples taken from your reading, studies, experience, or observations.

The New SAT Test

The new test rolls out Spring 2016 (with the new PSAT coming out in October 2015). You will find new practice questions available at collegeboard.com and Khan Academy has an entire suite of videos aimed at preparing students for the new test https://www.khanacademy.org/sat

The new test is supposed to be a more straightforward test than the earlier versions. Time will, of course, give us more insight.

SAT Subject Tests

In addition to the SAT Exam, you may also take a host of SAT Subject Tests. These are one-hour multiple-choice tests on a specific subject. There are currently 20 tests in English, history, math, science, and languages.

You will find that some colleges will require a minimum of three to five SAT Subject Tests. Some will dictate which ones, others will let you choose. This seems to be especially true for admitting a homeschooled student. You would be wise to check with your college of choice early on so that you're sure to take the correct tests on a timely basis.

Or, if there is an area in which you shine, taking the subject test is a great way to show this to a college admissions officer.

These tests are given on the same dates as the SAT and you may take up to three in one day. Go to www.collegeboard.com for additional information and to register for these tests.

PLAN® – ACT Preparation Test

Similar to the PSAT prep test for the SAT, PLAN® is designed to prepare students for taking the ACT. And like the PSAT, PLAN® is administered by local high schools, so you would need to contact a Guidance Counselor near you to make arrangements for your student to take this test. It is designed to be taken in a student's 10th grade year.

PLAN® goes another step beyond ACT test preparation though, as it helps students explore career and training options. If you have a student looking to enter the workforce upon graduation, this may be a test to consider. www.act.org/planstudent/

ACT (American College Testing Program)

Another college admissions test used by admissions officers is the ACT. This test is offered six times per year and provides a slightly different format and scoring system than the SAT.

Obviously different students will prefer one over the other. My daughter preferred the SAT and scored higher on it. Her friend preferred the ACT and her scores reflected it.

What's the difference? Students with stronger reading and grammar skills will probably prefer the ACT, while those with a strong vocabulary will do well on the SAT. And, if you're strong in math, the ACT may be the test for you as it goes into higher level math skills than the SAT.

It has been said that one of the goals of the new SAT rolling out in 2016 was to make it more like the ACT – that is with a more clear questioning format.

The ACT provides scores in four areas: English, Math, Reading and Science Reasoning. Each section receives a score from 1 to 36 points and these scores are averaged together for a composite score. As with the SAT, most colleges will take the highest score from each section of multiple tests and average them together to give you the highest possible composite score.

The ACT has an optional 30-minute Writing Test section which will measure your skills in planning and writing a short essay.

For information on registering for the ACT, go to www.actstudent.org. ACT fees begin at $38 and go up, depending upon which components you take and what scoring services you would like.

The SAT vs. the ACT

The Kaplan Test Prep website (www.kaptest.com) has a chart comparing the SAT and the ACT. You will find a portion of the chart on the following page.

In addition, Princeton Review offers an ACT/SAT Best Fit Live Online Quiz to help you determine whether you may do better on the ACT or SAT. Kaplan offers a SAT/ACT Combo Sample Test. From these assessments, you can determine which test may be best for you.

Be sure to check the requirements for the college you would like to attend to see if they require one over the other. If not – use the chart or one of the above assessments to help decide which test you'd like to take. *Or,* take both if you wish.

SAT/ACT Comparison Chart
Source: http://www.kaptest.com/college-prep/test-information/sat-vs-act

	ACT	SAT
Test Length	3 hours, 25 minutes (with Writing Test)	3 hours, 45 minutes
Test Structure	**4 Sections** English, Math, Reading, Science plus an optional Writing Test	**10 Sections** 3 Critical Reading, 3 Math, 3 Writing and 1 Experimental, which is unscored
Scoring	Composite of 1-36 based on average scores from 4 test sections ■ 4 scores of 1-36 for each test ■ Optional Writing Test score of 0-12 (not included in the overall score)	Total score range of 600-2400 based on adding scores from 3 subjects ■ 3 scores of 200-800 for each subject ■ Score of 0-12 for the Essay
Wrong Answer Penalty	No penalty for wrong answers	¼ point subtracted from your raw score for each wrong answer (except for Math Grid-ins)
Sending Score History	You decide which score is sent	You decide which score is sent *Some colleges require you to send all scores, check with the college to be sure
■ **Reading**	Reading Comprehension	Reading Comprehension Sentence Completions
■ **Math**	Arithmetic, algebra, geometry, algebra 2, trigonometry	Arithmetic, algebra, geometry and algebra 2
■ **Science**	Analysis, interpretation, evaluation, basic content, and problem solving	Not applicable
■ **Essay**	Optional Final Section ■ 30 minutes ■ Not included in composite score ■ Topic of importance to high school students	First Section ■ 25 minutes ■ Factored into overall score ■ More abstract topic

There is a restriction on the types of calculators you may use. Generally scientific or graphing calculators are okay. Be sure to have extra batteries.

P.E.R.T. - Postsecondary Education Readiness Test

Most colleges require an SAT or ACT score for admission. If a student's scores are weak in an area, the college may also require a college placement test to determine which classes a student will be placed in. You may usually take this test at the college's testing center, or you may find that some state colleges have given the responsibility to local high schools.

The P.E.R.T. provides assessment in three areas: Reading, Writing and Mathematics

Minimum test scores to be placed in college level classes are generally as follows:

Reading 106

Writing 103

Mathematics 114

Taking the Test!

Don't be afraid to take any of these tests more than once. Becoming familiar with the test and discovering your weak spots can only help improve your scores.

I recommend taking a combination of at least three tests – perhaps the SAT twice and the ACT once. You should plan to <u>finish</u> testing by the <u>beginning of your senior year</u> as you will need these test scores to meet certain scholarship and college application deadlines. There is nothing wrong with taking these tests well into your senior year to improve your college standing, but many scholarship and admissions deadlines come early in the year and will require test scores.

Keep in mind these general test-taking strategies:

- Know where the testing center is located and leave in plenty of time to get there early.
- Read the test's directions carefully.
- Eliminate choices on multiple choice questions.
- Be sure to fill in the correct bubbles on your answer sheet. It's easier to do if you work in blocks. For example, do questions 1-5 in your workbook, then transfer the answers to your score sheet.
- Don't spend too much time on any one question. Skip the hard ones, but come back to them at the end.
- Keep track of time during the test.
- Get plenty of rest the night before.
- Eat a good breakfast.
- Have plenty of pencils and batteries for your calculator.
- Wear comfortable clothing.
- Relax!

CLEP Tests (College-Level Examination Program)

This is **NOT** a college entrance test. The CLEP test evaluates your student's knowledge of a specific subject. If your student can obtain a certain score on the CLEP test, they can often obtain college credit for the course and will not have to take that course in college. Test scores are from 20 to 80 and 50 is considered passing for the majority of the tests. You will need to check with your college to see what their requirements are for earning CLEP credit.

There are about 33 subject-specific CLEP tests available to you. Because a CLEP score is good for several years, it is a good idea to take the CLEP as soon as you finish the corresponding course in high school so that the material is still fresh. You can, however, take the CLEP any time you are ready to do so – even while enrolled in college.

CLEP tests are offered at many testing centers – many of them on community college campuses. You can find a listing of the one nearest you at http://clep.collegeboard.org/search/test-centers

The tests cost about $80. If you compare this to the cost of actually taking the college course, you will find this is extremely economical.

CollegeBoard (www.collegeboard.com) offers CLEP test preparation booklets, as do many bookstores.

Other College Credit Exam Options

While many of us are familiar with the idea of a CLEP exam, there are other testing options for earning college credit.

DANTES Subject Standardized Tests (DSST Exam)
- Over 30 test titles
- Approximately $80 per test
- Accepted by over 2000 colleges
- www.getcollegecredit.com

Check out
www.4tests.com
for free practice tests.

Excelsior College Exams (ECE) and UExcel Exams
- Over 50 tests
- www.excelsior.edu – click on 'Credit by Exam'
- www.uexceltest.com

GED – General Educational Development Test

In order to achieve some of your continuing education goals, you may be required to take the GED. We all know that for some the GED carries a certain stigma with it, however, it still may be a course you wish to pursue. The internet lists Bill Cosby, Michael J. Fox, Peter Jennings, Dave Thomas and Mary Lou Retton among the list of famous people who have taken the GED to complete their high school education.

To obtain information on taking the GED, go to www.gedtestingservice.com
or contact your local school district or state college. A new, more challenging version of the test was released in 2014, and it is now given on computer rather than paper. You can find specific test information at www.gedtestingservice.com/educators/2014test.

You are expected to have at least a 9th grade reading level and will be tested on language arts, social studies, science and mathematical reasoning.

There are several preparation books to help you prepare for the GED – two popular sources are Barron's How to Prepare for the GED Test and Kaplan GED Test Strategies, Practice and Review.

CHAPTER 8 – APPLYING FOR TECHNICAL SCHOOLS, COLLEGES AND SCHOLARSHIPS

Choosing Your Destination

If your student is technical school or college bound, it is wise to begin researching options early in their high school years. In this way, you have a general direction and you can begin fulfilling entrance requirements early on.

What if you're not sure which colleges offer courses of study that interest your student?

Do you think Harvard is calling their name? How about Wheaton College? Ever considered Duke University? Or, would they enjoy the change of seasons at Vanderbilt University? Can you learn to program computers in Idaho?

Is there a college in New York that specializes in Air Mechanics? How about one in Hawaii that teaches Sports Medicine? Where's the best place to go to study Interior Decorating? What if your student wants to repair truck engines?

Well here are a few good places to start your search. To search colleges within the Florida University system, or to find vocational training around the state, go to Florida Virtual Campus as www.flvc.org.

If you would like to expand your search outside the state, try these search engines:

www.fastweb.com   (My personal favorite)
www.petersons.com
www.collegeboard.com

www.colleges.com

www.collegeview.com

It is also a great idea to attend any college fairs which come to your area. The National Association for College Admission Counseling (NACAC) offers college fairs all throughout the year. Go to www.nacacnet.org to see when the next one is coming to your area.

And then, just get online and look at colleges that sound interesting to you. Keep in mind that college website addresses will end with .edu rather than .com or .org.

When looking at schools, some things to pay attention to are:

- High school course requirements*
- Entrance test scores*
- Application deadlines
- References required
- Fees required
- Community service required
- Additional requirements for home-schooled students
- Out of state tuition differences

*Most college websites will list a minimum requirement for both test scores and credit requirements — but satisfying these requirements does not guarantee admission. Look for the statement that says what the typical accepted student has completed so that you know what your goal is. For example, you may find that even though the college requires four math credits, most accepted students actually had five.

When you are serious about a college or vocational school, take time to go visit. Call the visitor's office and schedule a tour of the campus. If you are relatively certain of an area of study, schedule an appointment with someone in that area as well.

When my daughter and I started visiting colleges, she had her heart set on one particular school, but I was concerned because I had the impression that they did not have a strong department for her desired course of study. When we met with the school officials, however I was surprised to learn that her particular area brought in more money for this school than their entire combined athletic department – and this is a MAJOR athletic school.

A visit will also give you a "feel" for the school and how your student will fit. Talk with as many people as possible while you are there. When you call the visitor's office, tell them what your interests are and they will advise you on who you should meet with and will help schedule appointments for you.

Friends of mine had their hearts set on a particular school, but when they visited, they discovered many school philosophies that differed greatly from their own. These were not evident from the school's material, but were quickly seen when they were face to face with school personnel.

If this is a college away from home, take a look at the housing arrangements, as well as the available meal plans. Most college websites will also have this information.

The Application

To begin the college application process, you generally start by completing the online application for your particular college of choice and pay the corresponding application fee. Some colleges take advantage of the Common Application found at commonapp.org while others require that you complete the application on their site.

Once the application is filed, you will also need to send some supporting documentation such as test scores, transcripts or an SSAR and perhaps letters of recommendation.

A couple of colleges in the state of Florida are asking applicants to complete the Self Reported Student Academic Record (SSAR) if they have not yet graduated from high school. It is a record of the high school and college courses you have completed or are currently taking along with the grades earned. You can find additional information at www.selfreportedtranscript.com/ssar. Check your college's website to see if this is a requirement.

What Does College Cost? And – How Do We Pay For It?

Okay, so now you know where you want to go to college (did you decide on Harvard or Emory?), let's talk about paying for it. Just what does a college education cost these days? Here are a few sample numbers for you to consider:

University	FL Resident Tuition	Other Fees	Housing & Meals	Other Costs	Total Cost per Year
Florida State University *Public university, Tallahassee, FL* www.fsu.edu	$6,512	$1,000	$10,208	$1,828	$19,548
Rollins College *Private university, Winter Park, FL* www.rollins.edu	$43,080	$5,450	$13,470	Included	$56,550
Wheaton College *Private – Illinois* www.wheaton.edu	$32,950		$9,290	$3,020	$45,260
University of North Carolina *Public – N. Carolina, Florida residents pay out of state tuition* www.uncw.edu	$18,054	$2,459	$9,862	$5,994	$36,369
Miami Dade College www.mdc.edu	$2,790				$2,790

Figures taken from college websites – 2015

There are many ways to pay for your college education – family money, money given to you, money you have earned and even borrowed money.

Prepaid Tuition and Education Savings Plans

The IRS allows you to save money in certain education savings plans for your children's college tuition and receive some tax benefits. In the state of Florida you may participate in the Florida Prepaid College Plan or the Florida 529 Savings Plan. Each plan has its benefits – one will allow you to lock in future rates and the other gives you a little more flexibility for use on the other end. Go to www.myfloridaprepaid.com for more information.

Scholarships

Florida Bright Futures Scholarship

www.floridastudentfinancialaid.org/SSFAD/bf/

Many Florida students will be relying on the Florida Bright Futures Scholarship for their college education. Listed below are the current requirements for homeschooled students– keep in mind that the Florida Legislature is authorized to change eligibility requirements each year, so be sure you are checking on the requirements each year – especially during your senior year.

Florida Academic Scholars (FAS):
- A best combined score of 1290 SAT or 29 ACT
- 100 community service hours
- Currently pays approximately $103 per hour for semester courses at a 4-year school

Florida Medallion Scholars (FMS):
- A best combined score of 1220 SAT or 27 ACT
- 75 community service hours

        OR

- A best combined score of 1170 SAT or 26 ACT
- A weighted 3.0 GPA in the required 16 college preparatory credits.
- 75 community service hours
- *This second option requires that your 16 core credits be validated via dual enrollment, FLVS or a public or private school transcript.*
- Currently pays approximately $77 per hour for semester courses at a 4-year school

All of these criteria must be met by high school graduation, and you should be aware that if you are registered with the county, Bright Futures will check to be sure you were registered as a homeschooler in **both** the 11th and 12th grades.

To be eligible to apply for a Bright Futures Scholarship, you must begin by submitting a complete Florida Financial Aid Application during your last year in high school. Go to www.floridastudentfinancialaid.org and apply online. This application is generally available online beginning January 1st. IF YOU DO NOT COMPLETE THIS APPLICATION PRIOR TO GRADUATION, YOU FORFEIT ALL FUTURE ELIGIBILITY FOR A BRIGHT FUTURES SCHOLARSHIP! (Although not required, you should also complete the FAFSA application – see the next section for complete information.)

If you are enrolled under a non-traditional private school, you will need to ask your school to submit your transcripts. The school can submit your transcripts online by the middle of your senior year. They will be responsible for getting all records to Tallahassee, so work closely with your school's administrator to be sure this is done.

Additional information on the Bright Futures Scholarships can be found at www.floridastudentfinancialaid.org/SSFAD/bf/.

A chart showing how awards are paid out can be found at
http://www.floridastudentfinancialaid.org/SSFAD/PDF/BFHandbookChapter2.pdf#page=5

Bright Futures Home Education manual

http://www.floridastudentfinancialaid.org/SSFAD/bf/pdf/BFHomeEdManual.pdf

Remember – check the websites often – especially at the beginning of the school year as legislative changes may alter the information printed in this book.

Other Scholarships

There IS money out there for college – the questions are:

"How do I find it? And, how do I get it offered to me?"

We are very fortunate to live in the age of the internet. Many websites offer scholarship searches. You will find a list of popular search engines on the following pages. But, if you're able to find these scholarships – so is everyone else in the country!

Keep in mind these facts:

- Fortunately, not everyone else in the country wants to go to college at the same time you do.
- Many scholarships offer multiple awards (for example, Burger King gave out approximately 1600 scholarships last year).
- The early bird often gets the worm – not everyone is working on this as early as you are!

You will find there are MANY, MANY scholarships out there. There are ones for members of nearly every ethnic group, ones for children of military families, ones for folks who live in the city, ones for folks who live on the farm, ones for left-handed students, ones for nearly every career pursuit out there, and so on, and so on.

Ways to increase your chances of winning:

- Apply for as many scholarships as possible.
- In fact – starting in your junior year or earlier, make it a point to apply for at least two scholarships a month. You can still apply for scholarships once you are in college – so this could be a good habit to maintain for a while.
- Don't pass by a scholarship just because the award is small – those $100 checks add up!
- Neatness and accuracy count!

You can locate potential scholarships at the following websites...

www.fastweb.com (Again, my personal favorite)
www.scholarships.com
www.collegeboard.com
www.petersons.com

You can also check with your local Chamber of Commerce and School Board to determine which local businesses give scholarships. Check with employers – both students' and parents', as several companies offer scholarships to employees. And, check with the college you are applying to, as they often have thousands, or even millions, of dollars they give to worthy students each year.

Start applying early. There are several scholarships and awards that can be applied for as young as age 13. And, don't wait until your senior year (but, if that's where you are now, it's still not too late!) Many scholarships have early deadlines – pay close attention to these requirements.

Other Ways to Pay for College

Grants

Grants are available to students who exhibit a financial need. And, grant money does not have to be repaid.

In order to qualify for a grant, students must complete the Free Application for Federal Student Aid (FAFSA) – www.fafsa.ed.gov. The application must be processed by the deadline established by the institution the student attends.

In order to renew the grant each year, students must generally maintain a minimum GPA in college and must apply each year.

You are generally notified of grants you are eligible for once you have completed the FAFSA and when you have been accepted to a college.

The state of Florida offers the *Florida Student Assistance Grant* along with a few other state-funded grants and scholarships. For more information go to www.FloridaStudentFinancialAid.org or call 1-888-827-2004.

Work Study

If students do not exhibit sufficient financial need to qualify for grants, they may still be eligible for a work study program. These programs are available on campus and allow a student to work for part of his or her tuition. They will be given a job in which their wages are applied towards their college finances.

Students, of course, are also free to find their own job and work their way through college.

Loans

And, finally, besides the free money (scholarships and grants) and the earned money (work study) – parents and/or students can also borrow money.

Loans are available from MANY different sources – some are government funded, some are from banks, etc. Once you have completed the FAFSA, or applied to a college, you will find information on college loans suddenly appearing in your mailbox.

Borrowing money for a college education can be an excellent investment. After all, if you borrow $20,000 to attend college and you are able to start a career making at least $10,000 more per year than you would have without your education – you will have recouped this amount, plus interest, in just three years.

But loans are just that – LOANS – and they must be repaid with interest. So – be wise when you borrow money. Look for the best interest rates and the best repayment plans available for your situation. ALWAYS pay more than the minimum monthly payment. The sooner you repay your loan, the less interest you will owe. And – do not borrow more than is necessary. After all – it's tradition for college students to live on a shoestring budget. ☺

IMPORTANT!!!

If you want any Florida money (including Bright Futures), you must file an application with the Office of Student Financial Assistance. This *does not* automatically apply for the Bright Futures – you must still file either through your non-traditional private school or as a homeschooled student at graduation time.

www.FloridaStudentFinancialAid.org

You should also complete the Free Application for Federal Student Aid (FAFSA) if you want to get any kind of student aid (including grants, loans and some scholarships). You can file online as early as January 1st of the year your student will enter college. File early!!

www.fafsa.ed.gov

NOTE: The FAFSA is a <u>free</u> application. If the website you are on charges you a fee – it's the wrong website!

PREPARING FOR COLLEGE CALENDAR

	Junior Year
June	• Arrange to take the PSAT with a local high school.
July	• Is dual enrollment for you? Look into taking a dual enrollment class at your community college this year.
September	• Review your credits and be sure you are on track to complete the required courses.
October	• Take the PSAT.
November	• Keep your grades up! • Start researching scholarships and grants for which you may be eligible. • Apply for two scholarships this month.
December	• Receive results from your PSAT. • Register for either the January ACT or SAT. • Apply for two scholarships this month. • Will you be dual enrolling for the spring semester?
January	• Make a list of colleges you would like to attend and investigate them. • Make arrangements to visit at least two this spring. • Take the ACT or SAT. • Apply for two scholarships this month.
February	• Request admission literature and financial aid information from colleges on your list. • Apply for two scholarships this month.
March	• Receive ACT or SAT results. • Arrange to take an SAT prep course if needed. • Select your senior courses. • Visit colleges. • Apply for two scholarships this month.
April	• Register for the May/June SAT Subject tests if you will need to take those. • Or, register for the ACT or SAT. • Keep your grades up! • Apply for any summer jobs you may want. • OR, arrange to volunteer this summer. • Apply for two scholarships this month.
May	• Take the SAT or SAT Subject Tests. • Apply for two scholarships this month.
June	• Take the ACT or SAT. • If you're working this summer, save some of that money in your college fund. • Apply for two scholarships this month. • Prepare your transcript through the end of your junior year.
July	• Choose which colleges you will officially apply to. • Gather the necessary information for your applications. • Draft your application essays. • Request letters of recommendation. • If you would like to play a sport in college, contact the coaches at the schools to which you are applying and ask about their sports program and their sports scholarships. • Start the NCAA process if you need to. • Will you be dual enrolling this year? • Apply for two scholarships this month.
August	• Submit your college applications. Be sure to include all required documentation and appropriate fees. • Keep copies of everything you submit. • Apply for two scholarships this month.

Senior Year	
September	• Be sure you are on track to complete all necessary credits for graduation. • You should have a *strong senior schedule* – just because you've met most of your criteria, it's no reason to coast. • Register to take the SAT or ACT one more time – do any necessary preparations to assure an improved score. • Be sure to have your test scores sent to the colleges you want to receive them. • Do you need to take any SAT Subject tests? • Apply for two scholarships this month.
October	• If you are applying for Early Action or Early Decision, your deadline is probably this month. • Apply for two scholarships this month.
November	• Maintain those grades! First semester grades are important to your college. • Keep up with all the paperwork coming from your college. • Apply for housing as soon as you are accepted by a college – this often includes making a deposit of several hundred dollars. • Again, keep copies of everything you submit. • Apply for two scholarships this month.
December	• If you applied for early decision, you will have an answer this month. • If you are accepted, you must withdraw all other college applications. • Enroll for any dual enrollment courses for your final semester. • Apply for two scholarships this month.
January	• Update your transcript. • Send a copy to the colleges to which you applied. • Keep up your grades! • Be sure you have completed the Florida Financial Aid application online. • Complete the FAFSA online as soon as possible. *Remember – first come, first served.* • Submit the necessary information for the Florida Bright Futures scholarship
February	• If you now have all your tax information, make any necessary corrections to your FAFSA. • Don't catch senioritis just yet. • Look one more time for any scholarships you may have missed.
March	• Review your college acceptances and financial aid awards. • Decide which college you will attend and notify everyone accordingly. • Submit any requested paperwork to your college of choice.
April	• Don't coast just yet – keep up those grades! • See any more scholarships?
May	• GRADUATE!
June	• Send your final transcript to your college and any scholarships that may require it. • Prepare for college orientation. • If you work this summer – save your money!

Sources: www.nacacnet.org and Cap & Gown magazine

CHAPTER 9 – THE FUN STUFF
Graduation and Senior Class "Stuff"

You have finally reached your senior year and it's time to celebrate all of your hard work. There are many ways to mark this milestone and you'll want to take advantage of many of them!

Senior Pictures

At the beginning of your senior year, you will want to have your senior picture made. This can range from the traditional tuxedo/drape picture done in a professional studio to a casual picture taken in a special setting.

Whatever the look, you will find that you have need of a senior picture for many events. Church bulletins, support groups, graduation ceremonies, family and friends all want a senior picture. Be sure to order several copies and have access to having more made in the event you didn't order enough.

Public schools typically set aside a particular studio for students to use so that their pictures are included in a yearbook. As homeschoolers, we have great freedom to choose. Prestige Portraits (prestigeportraits.com) is a nationwide firm that specializes in senior pictures – or you can shop around.

Be sure to check out your photographer's reviews and prices as these are special photos. You will want to have your photos done in the fall so that your pictures will be ready when you need them.

Class Rings and Momentos

Not too many folks wear class rings these days, but you may want to purchase some lasting momentos with the year on them to commemorate the occasion.

If you do want class rings, you can find them through jewelry websites such as Jostens (www.jostens.com), Herff Jones (www.herff-jones.com) or Balfour (www.balfour.com). Most students order their class ring during their junior year so that they can wear it their entire senior year. You may want to look into this early so that you can budget for this expense.

Ceremonies

Graduation is the culmination of all those years of hard work, so CELEBRATE!!

Many local support groups will hold graduations, or you may find a larger one in your area that will allow you to participate. Just be sure that it is a ceremony that fits with your family's lifestyle and desires for a graduation.

There is a state-wide graduation annually at the Florida Parent Educators Association's Florida Homeschool Convention held in May. Information on their graduation is generally available on their website (www.fpea.com) in the fall. You will need to sign up early to be able to participate. This has been a beautiful, classy event from the beginning, so if you will be in the area, it may be something special you want to take advantage of.

In most graduation ceremonies, graduates are responsible for obtaining their own cap and gown. Some ceremonies will require a certain color, while others will allow you to choose. Two of our local events allow the students to vote for the "color of the year" and then everyone is required to wear that color. The FPEA Graduation ceremony generally allows students to wear their own colors – making for a very colorful event.

Caps and gowns can be obtained from several sources. Some very popular ones are Jostens (www.jostens.com), Herff Jones (www.herff-jones.com) and Graduation Source (www.graduationsource.com).

Many ceremonies will allow you to present a list of your student's accomplishments as part of the presentation. Some have the parents presenting the diploma and some will have a distinguished guest making the presentations.

On the other hand, while many students do wish to take advantage of organized graduation ceremonies, many others celebrate with a family-planned party. You may wish to throw a big party and invite all the friends and relatives. You can even choose to have someone pronounce a blessing over your child as they prepare to enter a new phase of their life.

For a special memento, prepare a scrapbook of pictures of them growing up and then have friends and family add their comments.

Graduation Announcements

Whether you participate in a large ceremony or not, you will still want to send announcements letting EVERYONE know that your child is graduating. Some organized ceremonies will have announcements available for you to order – otherwise you will need to obtain them yourself.

Local printers have many to choose from, or you may wish to design your own with your computer.

It is with great pleasure that we announce the Graduation of

Jonathan Edward Banks

On Saturday evening, May 27, 2017 Steubenville, Ohio

~~~~~~

"Go light your world."

(PC Font – Brush Script BT)

Having been diligently taught at home, it is now time to celebrate with us the graduation of

Jennifer Ann Crawford

Class of 2021

With honor, we invite you to attend her graduation on Saturday, May 27, 2021 At 7:00 p.m. Main Street Church

Mighty oaks from small acorns grow.

(PC Font – Edwardian Script ITC)

If you are participating in a Graduation Ceremony, be sure to differentiate between graduation <u>announcements</u> and <u>invitations</u> to the ceremony.

<u>Diplomas</u>

If you will be designing your own diploma, here is a sample you may wish to follow.
Feel free to design your own.

Sample

Jackson Academy

Be it known that

Andrew Jackson

Having satisfactorily met the requirements for graduation is awarded this

Diploma

*In testimony whereof, we have hereby set our signatures
On this thirtieth day of May, 2017.*

_____   _____

Principal   *Teacher*

They will be called oaks of righteousness, a planting of the Lord for the display of his splendor.

(PC Fonts – Brush Script BT and Old English Text MT)

Either frame your diploma, or enclose it in a diploma cover.   Jostens, Herff Jones,
Graduation Source and many others offer diploma covers.   You can search the internet
for diploma covers and find some very nice ones.

Celebrations

Throughout the course of your senior year, you will have the opportunity to celebrate in many ways. Here are just a few of the organized events you may wish to take advantage of:

- Walt Disney World

    Rather than its Grad Night in previous years, WDW now provides senior class trips. Get a group of seniors together and arrange a special trip any time of the year. Disney will even arrange rooms, meals, dessert receptions or parties if you would like them.

    For more information call 1-877-WD-YOUTH (1-877-939-6884) or visit disneyseniorclasstrip.com. Make plans early, reservations are required.

- Grad Bash at Universal Islands of Adventure

    Held on several nights in April and May from about 7 p.m. to 2 a.m.
    Unlimited access to the park, concerts
    Dress Code
    Additional activities available outside the park

    For more information call 1-800-761-2556 or visit gradbash.com

    You can also get information on these and other events at
    www.grad-nights.com
    1-800-544-7646

- Jr/Sr Proms and Dinners

    Many local groups offer some form of Jr/Sr Prom or Dinner. Check with your local support group. (One way to find your local support group is through the FPEA website – www.fpea.com)

- <u>Senior Trips</u>

    Take, or send, your student on a special trip somewhere. Perhaps a cruise, a trip to New York City, or just a weekend away for your student can make for a memorable occasion.

Whatever you choose to do for your senior in this very special year – just be sure to celebrate. It has taken many years and lots of hard work to get to this point. Honor that hard work!

FORMS

Forms Index

Personal Information

This is a place to gather general information that you may need when completing college or scholarship applications. Use the additional blank spaces to record unique information about yourself.

Student Information

Full name	Date of birth

Current Address

City	State	Zip	Primary phone

Student Email	Secondary phone

Parent Email	

Additional Info

Career Ideas

If you could be anything you wanted when you grow up – what would it be?

Top Three Career Choice Ideas

1)

2)

3)

College or Training Needed

List the college education or training that you think you would need to achieve your goals.

Interesting article:
http://lifehacker.com/four-ways-to-figure-out-what-you-really-want-to-do-with-513095544

Note that there is no space for your social security number. You may still be asked to provide that for some college applications, but for security reasons, I encourage you not to put that on any forms unless specifically asked to do so.

High School Information

Public or Private Schools Attended

Name of School Attended			Contact Phone
Address			
City	State	Zip	Website or email contact
Contact Person		I have my records from this school	☐ YES ☐ NO

Name of School Attended			Contact Phone
Address			
City	State	Zip	Website or email contact
Contact Person		I have my records from this school	☐ YES ☐ NO

Private School Coverings

Name of School Attended			Contact Phone
Address			
City	State	Zip	Website or email contact
Contact Person		I have my records from this school	☐ YES ☐ NO

Name of School Attended			Contact Phone
Address			
City	State	Zip	Website or email contact
Contact Person		I have my records from this school	☐ YES ☐ NO

Registered with the County

County Supervisor			Annual results sent:
Address			☐ 9th grade
			☐ 10th grade
City	State	Zip	☐ 11th grade
			☐ 12th grade
Phone	Email		☐ Termination notice sent upon graduation

Work Experience

Organization	Dates of Employment
Address	Phone
City	State	Zip	Supervisor's Name
Special training received	Your position
	Promotions received

Skills gained at this job

Organization	Dates of Employment
Address	Phone
City	State	Zip	Supervisor's Name
Special training received	Your position
	Promotions received

Skills gained at this job

Organization	Dates of Employment
Address	Phone
City	State	Zip	Supervisor's Name
Special training received	Your position
	Promotions received

Skills gained at this job

Volunteering

Organization name	Dates served
Address	Website

City	State	Zip	Phone or email

Supervisor's name	Verification letter obtained (on organization letterhead)
Type of work done	☐ YES ☐ NO
	Total number of hours served:

Organization name	Dates served
Address	Website

City	State	Zip	Phone or email

Supervisor's name	Verification letter obtained (on organization letterhead)
Type of work done	☐ YES ☐ NO
	Total number of hours served:

Organization name	Dates served
Address	Website

City	State	Zip	Phone or email

Supervisor's name	Verification letter obtained (on organization letterhead)
Type of work done	☐ YES ☐ NO
	Total number of hours served:

Organization name	Dates served
Address	Website

City	State	Zip	Phone or email

Supervisor's name	Verification letter obtained (on organization letterhead)
Type of work done	☐ YES ☐ NO
	Total number of hours served:

Log of Volunteer Hours

Keep track of your total number of volunteer hours with this form. Us the more comprehensive volunteer form to keep track of details.

Student Name:

Date(s) Served	Organization Served	Supervisor's Name	Verification Form Obtained?	Hours Served
			☐	
			☐	
			☐	
			☐	
			☐	
			☐	
			☐	
			☐	
			☐	
			☐	
			☐	
			☐	
			☐	
			☐	
			☐	
			☐	
			☐	
			☐	

Sample Volunteer Service Hour Letter

To be printed on the service organization's letterhead

Date:

To Whom It May Concern:

This is to certify that **STUDENT NAME** has completed ### of service hours on this DATE(s).

Briefly describe the type of work done by the student.

_____

Signature from Organization Served

_____

Title

Clubs & Student Organizations

List clubs that you participated in. Example: 4H, Robotics, etc.

Name of Organization	Purpose of Organization
Address	
City / State / Zip	Contact Person
Website	Contact Phone
Positions held	Dates Participated

Name of Organization	Purpose of Organization
Address	
City / State / Zip	Contact Person
Website	Contact Phone
Positions held	Dates Participated

Name of Organization	Purpose of Organization
Address	
City / State / Zip	Contact Person
Website	Contact Phone
Positions held	Dates Participated

Name of Organization	Purpose of Organization
Address	
City / State / Zip	Contact Person
Website	Contact Phone
Positions held	Dates Participated

Sports Played

Sport Played	Years(s) played (dates)
Team Name	Head Coach
Organization or School	Coach Contact Info
Website	
Position(s) played	Team records (W/L)
	Individual achievements

Sport Played	Years(s) played (dates)
Team Name	Head Coach
Organization or School	Coach Contact Info
Website	
Position(s) played	Team records (W/L)
	Individual achievements

Sport Played	Years(s) played (dates)
Team Name	Head Coach
Organization or School	Coach Contact Info
Website	
Position(s) played	Team records (W/L)
	Individual achievements

Awards Won

Award Name	Date earned
Reason for earning award	Contact Person
Organization giving award	

Award Name	Date earned
Reason for earning award	Contact Person
Organization giving award	

Award Name	Date earned
Reason for earning award	Contact Person
Organization giving award	

Award Name	Date earned
Reason for earning award	Contact Person
Organization giving award	

Award Name	Date earned
Reason for earning award	Contact Person
Organization giving award	

Award Name	Date earned
Reason for earning award	Contact Person
Organization giving award	

Award Name	Date earned
Reason for earning award	Contact Person
Organization giving award	

Award Name	Date earned
Reason for earning award	Contact Person
Organization giving award	

Work Experience Evaluation

This form can be used as a portfolio tool to help track general skills needed in a work environment.

Student name	Date evaluation completed
Organization name	Date student employed
Evaluation completed by	Title

PERFORMS DESIGNATED JOB SKILLS	Always	Almost Always	Most of the Time	Almost Never	Never
Applies safety procedures while on the job.	☐	☐	☐	☐	☐
Displays an acceptable level of productivity and quality control.	☐	☐	☐	☐	☐
Demonstrates appropriate dress and grooming habits.	☐	☐	☐	☐	☐
Reacts to feedback in a positive manner.	☐	☐	☐	☐	☐
Communicates effectively with customers, co-workers, and management.	☐	☐	☐	☐	☐
Demonstrates decision-making and problem-solving skills.	☐	☐	☐	☐	☐
Demonstrates punctuality and reliability by working as scheduled.	☐	☐	☐	☐	☐
Demonstrates pride in work by completing work correctly and quickly.	☐	☐	☐	☐	☐
Demonstrates flexibility and the ability to perform a wide range of functions.	☐	☐	☐	☐	☐

DEMONSTRATES COMPLIANCE WITH WORK ETHICS	Always	Almost Always	Most of the Time	Almost Never	Never
Demonstrates integrity and honesty.	☐	☐	☐	☐	☐
Demonstrates interest, enthusiasm, and loyalty.	☐	☐	☐	☐	☐
Demonstrates ability to follow directions.	☐	☐	☐	☐	☐
Demonstrates ability to work cooperatively with team members and supervisors from different cultural backgrounds.	☐	☐	☐	☐	☐
Demonstrates an ability to follow written and oral directions.	☐	☐	☐	☐	☐
Displays a positive attitude toward the job.	☐	☐	☐	☐	☐
Practices cost effectiveness with company resources.	☐	☐	☐	☐	☐

Four Year Educational Plan

This form lists the courses students in Florida public schools need to graduate. Homeschoolers are not required to follow this exact course of study, but it is a good guideline for planning your high school years. Fill this form out in pencil and use it as your flexible guide over the next four years.

Full Name

Anticipated Graduation Year

High School Courses Taken Prior to 9th Grade

List any high school classes that you have taken prior to 9th grade. Many colleges will let you count these towards your college application credits. Be sure that the work that you have done is high school level – and keep it in your high school portfolio.

YEAR TAKEN	COURSE TITLE		CREDIT

REQUIRED SUBJECT AREAS	GRADE 9 Course Title	Gr.	Cr.	GRADE 10 Course Title	Gr.	Cr.	GRADE 11 Course Title	Gr.	Cr.	GRADE 12 Course Title	Gr.	Cr.
English Language Arts (4) *3 with substantial writing*												
Mathematics (4) *Algebra 1 & higher if college bound*												
Science (3) *Incl. Biology & 2 equally rigorous courses. 2 w/lab*												
Social Studies (3) *1 U.S. History 0.5 U.S. Gov 1 World History 0.5 Economics w/Fin'l Lit*												
World Language *Not req'd for graduation, but 2 credits in same language req'd for college admission*												
Physical Education (1)												
Fine & Performing Arts, Speech & Debate or Practical Arts (1)												
Electives – *at least three more strong academic credits.*												

Courses listed below the double line are not required on most college applications – however, they do add to a student's competitiveness. If you are college bound, be sure to add academic electives to your plan

OFFICIAL TRANSCRIPT

STUDENT INFORMATION

Full Name:		DOB:		Anticipated Grad Date:
Address:		Student ID#:		Graduation Date:
Email Address:		Gender:		Parents' Names:
		Phone:		

COURSE INFORMATION

Course #	Course Title	Subject Area	GR	CR	GPA	Course #	Course Title	Subject Area	GR	CR	GPA

Prior School Information

Dates	Name & Address

College Entrance Test Scores

Test	Date Taken	Scores

CUMULATIVE SUMMARY

Comm Svc Hrs	
Total Credits	
Unweighted GPA	
Weighted GPA	

Note: Honors, AP and Dual Enrollment courses are weighted on a half-point scale

Signed: _____ Date: _____

OFFICIAL TRANSCRIPT

STUDENT INFORMATION

Full Name:	DOB:	Anticipated Grad Date:
Address:	Student ID#:	
	Gender:	Graduation Date:
Email Address:	Phone:	Parents' Names:

ACADEMIC RECORD

COURSE/CLASS TITLE	Date Completed	Credits	Grade	GPA	COURSE/CLASS TITLE	Date Completed	Credits	Grade	GPA

PREVIOUS SCHOOLS ATTENDED

Name of School	Street Address	From	To

CUMULATIVE SUMMARY

TOTAL CREDITS	NON-WEIGHTED GPA	WEIGHTED GPA

Note: Honors, AP and Dual Enrollment courses are weighted on a half-point scale.

Signed: _____   Date: _____

OFFICIAL TRANSCRIPT

STUDENT INFORMATION

Full Name:	DOB:
Address:	Student ID#:
	Gender:
Email Address:	Phone:
	Anticipated Grad Date:
	Graduation Date:
	Parents' Names:

ACADEMIC RECORD

COURSE/CLASS TITLE	Date Completed	Credits	Grade	GPA
1200310 Algebra 1	6/2023	1.0	A	4.0
2109310 World History	6/2023	1.0	A	4.0
1001320 English 1 Hon.	6/2023	1.0	A	4.5
2003310 Physical Sci.	6/2023	1.0	A	4.0
0113300 Drafting 1	6/2023	1.0	A	
8209020 Bus Systems Tech	6/2023	1.0	A	
1900310 Drivers Ed w/ Lab	1/2024	0.5	A	
0800300 Health 1 Life Mgmt	1/2024	0.5	A	
1200330 Algebra 2	6/2024	1.0	B	
2000320 Biology 1 Hon.	6/2024	1.0	A	
1001340 English 2	6/2024	0.5	B	
2102310 Economics	6/2024	1.0	A	
1303300 Chorus 1	6/2024	0.5	A	
0104340 Drawing	6/2024	0.5	A	
0800330 Pers/Soc/Fam Rel.	6/2024	0.5	B	

COURSE/CLASS TITLE	Date Completed	Credits	Grade	GPA
2106310 American Gov't	12/2024	0.5	A	2.0
FRE1120 Beg French I	12/2024	1.0	A	4.5
1001370 English III	06/2025	1.0	A	4.0
2003350 Chemistry I Hnrs	06/2025	1.0	A	4.5
...0310 American History	06/2025	1.0	A	4.0
...C2010 Int'd Prin Bio	05/2025	1.0	A	4.5
FRE1121 Beg French 2	05/2025	1.0	A	4.5
...0 Softball	05/2025	0.5	A	2.0
ENC... English Comp 1	12/2025	1.0	A	4.5
...College Algebra	12/2025	1.0	A	4.5
...in of Bio 2	12/2025	1.0	B	3.5
...onal Fitness	12/2025	0.5	A	2.0
...cs Honors	05/2026			
...us 2	05/2026			
ENC... ...Comp 2	05/2026			
HUM22.. Lit. 15th/20th	05/2026			
...Elem Statistics	05/2026			

PREVIOUS SCHOOLS ATTENDED

Name of School	Street Address		From	To
River Christian	446 Water Street	Orlando, FL 32804	9-2020	6-2022

CUMULATIVE SUMMARY

TOTAL CREDITS	NON-WEIGHTED GPA	WEIGHTED GPA
23.0	3.85	4.04

Signed: _____   Date: _____

Note: Honors, AP and Dual Enrollment courses are weighted on a half-point scale.

How to Calculate Your Grade Point Average (GPA)

There are several GPA scales available and every college will use their own to recalculate your GPA once you submit your transcript. But you should include both a weighted and unweighted GPA on your transcript.

In order to show that work done in certain courses is more rigorous, you may choose to weight those grades. The typical grade point scale is the 4.0 scale in which As receive 4 points, Bs receive 3, etc. A half-point weighted scale will add a half point to your GPA. A full-point scale will add one point to your grades. Typically only As, Bs and Cs are weighted – not Ds or Fs for obvious reasons. If the course only receives a half-credit, you would also need to divide your GPA by half.

My recommendation is that students use the half-point scale. In this way, should a college use a different scale, they end up bringing your GPA up – not down. No sad surprises.

UNWEIGHTED Quality Points			HALF-POINT WEIGHTED Qualify Points			FULL POINT WEIGHTED Quality Points		
Letter Grade	For a Half credit	For a Full credit	Letter Grade	For a Half credit	For a Full credit	Letter Grade	For a Half credit	For a Full credit
A	2.0	4.0	A	2.25	4.5	A	2.5	5.0
B	1.5	3.0	B	1.75	3.5	B	2.0	4.0
C	1.0	2.0	C	1.25	2.5	C	1.5	3.0
D	0.5	1.0	D	0.5	1.0	D	0.5	1.0
F	0.0	0.0	F	0.0	0.0	F	0.0	0.0

Even if you have only one weighted course in your calculations – that is now your weighted GPA. To calculate the unweighted version, simply remove the extra half (or full) point and recalculate. You will want to calculate a cumulative GPA only – not a separate one for each year. So, simply total all high school credits and all grade points and find the overall average.

Note on the **sample transcript** on page 112 that some classes earned 4.5 GPA quality points for an A, and 3.5 GPA quality points for a B. This is because they are advanced courses and may be weighted. (See chapter 3.) Now, let's look at how the weighted and unweighted GPAs were calculated:

First – we total the number of credits: 23
Then – we add the number of GPA quality points: 93
Now – we divide the total number of GPA points by the total number of credits: 93/23=4.04
The weighted GPA is 4.04

In order to calculate the unweighted GPA, we will have to reduce the weighted points to an unweighted value – As get 4.0, Bs get 3.0, etc.

Total of the unweighted points: 88.5
Divide total unweighted GPA quality points by total number of credits: 88.5/23=3.85
The unweighted GPA is 3.85

Sample High School Resume
Student Name
March 2019

Test Scores and GPA
    ACT (10/26/09)   23
    SAT (Mar 09) 1700
    Weighted GPA: 4.08
    Unweighted GPA: 3.86

Honors Classes
    English I Honors (A)
    Biology I Honors (A)
    Physics Honors (currently enrolled – first semester grade – A)

Dual Enrollment Classes (*Valencia Community College*)
    FRE 1120 Beginning French I (A)
    FRE 1121 Beginning French II (A)
    BSC 2010C Principles of Biology I (A)
    ENC 1101 English Comp I (A)
    MAC 1105 College Algebra (A)
    BSC 2011C Principles of Biology II (B)
    ENC 1102 English Comp II (currently enrolled)
    HUM 2236 Humanities 15th/20th Centuries (currently enrolled)

Extracurricular Activities:
    Youth Choir – Main Street Church (2016 – present)
    Softball – Angels (fast pitch) short stop
    Softball – Lady Challengers (slow pitch) short stop/center field
    Baptist Campus Ministries – Valencia Community College

Community Involvement:
    March Madness – community service projects (March 2018)
    Impact the City – community service projects (June 2017)
    Habitat for Humanity (Summer 2017)
    Mom & Pops (mentoring younger teens) – Main Street Church (Sept 2018 – present)

Employment:
    R.O.C.K. Solid Christian Bookstore (April 2016 – October 2017)
    Still work conventions annually with R.O.C.K. Solid
    Chick-fil-A *Crew Member* (November 2017 – September 2018)
    Chick-fil-A *Crew Leader* (August 2018 – present)

Awards:
    Science Fair Project – 2nd place in regional homeschool fair (9th grade)
    Writer's Award for research paper on John Glenn (9th grade)
    President's List, Valencia Community College, Spring Term, 2019
    Earned Food Management Certificate – August 2019
    Dean's List, Valencia Community College – Fall Term 2019

TAB INSERTS FOR 8-TAB DIVIDER SETS

ENGLISH 1	ENGLISH 1	ALGEBRA 1	ALGEBRA 1
ENGLISH 2	ENGLISH 2	ALGEBRA 2	ALGEBRA 2
ENGLISH 3	ENGLISH 3	GEOMETRY	GEOMETRY
ENGLISH 4	ENGLISH 4	PRE-CALCULUS	PRE-CALCULUS
AMERICAN LIT	AMERICAN LIT	CALCULUS	CALCULUS
BRITISH LIT	BRITISH LIT	TRIGONOMETRY	TRIGONOMETRY
ENGLISH COMPOSITION	ENGLISH COMPOSITION	U.S. HISTORY	U.S. HISTORY
LITERATURE	LITERATURE	WORLD HISTORY	WORLD HISTORY
PHYSICAL SCIENCE	PHYSICAL SCIENCE	ECONOMICS	ECONOMICS
BIOLOGY	BIOLOGY	U.S. GOVERNMENT	U.S. GOVERNMENT
CHEMISTRY	CHEMISTRY	SOCIAL STUDIES	SOCIAL STUDIES
PHYSICS	PHYSICS	GEOGRAPHY	GEOGRAPHY
EARTH SCIENCE	EARTH SCIENCE	POLITICAL SCIENCE	POLITICAL SCIENCE
MARINE SCIENCE	MARINE SCIENCE	HUMANITIES	HUMANITIES
ART	ART	SPANISH 1	SPANISH 1
MUSIC	MUSIC	SPANISH 2	SPANISH 2
DRAMA	DRAMA	FRENCH 1	FRENCH 1
PHYSICAL EDUCATION	PHYSICAL EDUCATION	FRENCH 2	FRENCH 2
DRIVER'S ED	DRIVER'S ED	SIGN LANGUAGE 1	SIGN LANGUAGE 1
HEALTH	HEALTH	SIGN LANGUAGE 2	SIGN LANGUAGE 2

BLANK TAB INSERTS FOR 8-TAB DIVIDER SETS

TAB INSERTS FOR 5-TAB DIVIDER SETS

ENGLISH 1	ENGLISH 1	ALGEBRA 1	ALGEBRA 1
ENGLISH 2	ENGLISH 2	ALGEBRA 2	ALGEBRA 2
ENGLISH 3	ENGLISH 3	GEOMETRY	GEOMETRY
ENGLISH 4	ENGLISH 4	PRE-CALCULUS	PRE-CALCULUS
AMERICAN LIT	AMERICAN LIT	CALCULUS	CALCULUS
BRITISH LIT	BRITISH LIT	TRIGONOMETRY	TRIGONOMETRY
ENGLISH COMPOSITION	ENGLISH COMPOSITION	AMERICAN HISTORY	AMERICAN HISTORY
LITERATURE	LITERATURE	WORLD HISTORY	WORLD HISTORY
PHYSICAL SCIENCE	PHYSICAL SCIENCE	ECONOMICS	ECONOMICS
BIOLOGY	BIOLOGY	AMERICAN GOVERNMENT	AMERICAN GOVERNMENT
CHEMISTRY	CHEMISTRY	SOCIAL STUDIES	SOCIAL STUDIES
PHYSICS	PHYSICS	GEOGRAPHY	GEOGRAPHY
EARTH SCIENCE	EARTH SCIENCE	POLITICAL SCIENCE	POLITICAL SCIENCE
MARINE SCIENCE	MARINE SCIENCE	HUMANITIES	HUMANITIES
ART	ART	SPANISH 1	SPANISH 1
MUSIC	MUSIC	SPANISH 2	SPANISH 2
DRAMA	DRAMA	FRENCH 1	FRENCH 1
PHYSICAL EDUCATION	PHYSICAL EDUCATION	FRENCH 2	FRENCH 2
DRIVER'S ED	DRIVER'S ED	SIGN LANG. 1	SIGN LANG. 1
HEALTH	HEALTH	SIGN LANG. 2	SIGN LANG. 2

BLANK TAB INSERTS FOR 5-TAB DIVIDER SETS

RESOURCES

STATE OF FLORIDA HIGH SCHOOL INFORMATION

Curriculum Course Codes and Descriptions
www.cpalms.org/courses/coursedescriptionsearch.aspx

Florida Bright Futures – homeschool info
http://www.floridastudentfinancialaid.org/SSFAD/bf/pdf/
BFHomeEdManual.pdf

Florida Bright Futures Scholarship
www.floridastudentfinancialaid.org/SSFAD/bf/
1-888-827-2004

Florida Department of Education
www.fldoe.org

Florida Financial Aid Application
www.floridastudentfinancialaid.org
1-888-827-2004

Florida State Statutes
www.leg.state.fl.us/

Florida Virtual School
www.flvs.net
800-374-1430

Florida Workforce Education Frameworks
www.fldoe.org/workforce/dwdframe/

CURRICULUM RESOURCES

ABeka Books
www.abeka.com
1-877-223-5226

Apologia Curriculum
www.apologia.com
1-888-524-4724

Bob Jones University Press
www.bjupress.com
1-800-845-5731

Calvert School
www.calvertschool.org
1-410-243-6054

**Central Christian Academy/
Academic Christ Centered Educational Services**
www.acces-inc.com
1-800-854-5840

Florida Virtual School
www.flvs.net
800-374-1430

Home Science Tools
Science lab equipment
www.homesciencetools.com
1-800-860-6272

National Driver Training
www.nationaldrivertraining.com
1-800-942-2050

R.O.C.K. Solid
www.rocksolidinc.com
1-800-705-3452

ADVANCED CURRICULUM INFORMATION

AICE Information
www.cie.org.uk

International Baccalaureate Organization
www.ibo.org
1-301-202-3000

AP Information
http://apcentral.collegeboard.com/home
1-888-225-5427

SAT Registration and more
AP/CLEP/SAT/PSAT/College/Scholarships
www.collegeboard.com
1-212-713-8000
Southern Regional Office: 1-866-392-4088

CHILD LABOR PARTIAL WAIVER

Department of Business and Professional Regulation
http://www.myfloridalicense.com/dbpr/reg/documents/WaiverApplicationDBPRFCL1002.pdf
1-850-488-3131

TESTING

ACT
500 ACT Drive
P.O. Box 168
Iowa City, IA   52243-0168
319-337-1270
www.actstudent.org

BJ Home Education Services
Customer Services
1700 Wade Hampton Blvd.
Greenville, SC   26914-0062
1-800-845-5731
www.bjup.com/services/testing/

CLEP Testing Centers
http://clep.collegeboard.org
1-800-257-9558

DSST
College credit by examination
www.getcollegecredit.com
1-877-471-9860

GED Testing with FL DOE
ged.fldoe.org
1-850-245-0449

GED Practice Tests
www.4tests.com

PSAT
www.collegeboard.com/psat
1-866-433-7728

SAT
www.collegeboard.com
1-212-713-8000
Florida office – 850-521-4900

TEST PREPARATION

Accuplacer Test Practice Questions
www.testprepreview.com/accuplacer_practice.htm

Kaplan
www.kaptest.com
1-800-KAP-TEST

College Prep Genius
www.collegeprepgenius.com
81-SAT-2-PREP (817-282-7737)

Princeton Review
www.princetonreview.com
1-800-2REVIEW (1-800-273-8439)

COLLEGES

College Searches
www.fastweb.com
www.petersons.com
www.collegeboard.com
www.colleges.com

Florida Pre-paid College Plan
www.myfloridaprepaid.com
1-800-552-GRAD (4723)

**National Association for College
Admission Counseling
(college fairs)**
www.nacacnet.org

SCHOLARSHIPS

Florida Bright Futures Scholarship
www.floridastudentfinancialaid.org/SSFAD/bf/
1-888-827-2004

Florida Bright Futures – homeschool info
http://www.floridastudentfinancialaid.org/SSFAD/bf/pdf/
BFHomeEdManual.pdf

Florida Financial Aid Application
www.floridastudentfinancialaid.org
1-888-827-2004

Scholarships for Volunteering
www.finaid.org/otheraid/service.phtml

Scholarship Searches *(these are just a
few – there are LOADS out there)*
www.fastweb.com
www.scholarships.com
www.collegeboard.com
www.petersons.com
www.careersandcolleges.com

**Free Application for Federal Student
Aid (FAFSA)**
www.fafsa.ed.gov
1-800-433-3243

GRADUATION SUPPIES

Balfour
www.balfour.com
1-800-Balfour (225-3687)

Graduation Source
www.graduationsource.com
800-352-6162
Herff-Jones
www.herff-jones.com

HomeSchool Grad Stuff
www.homeschoolgradstuff.com

Jostens
www.jostens.com

CELEBRATIONS

Disney Senior Class Trips
www.disneyseniorclasstrip.com
1-877-WD-YOUTH

Universal Islands of Adventure Grad Bash
www.universalorlando.com/Events/Grad-Bash.aspx
1-800-YOUTH-15

Additional Grad Nite info
www.grad-nights.com
1-800-544-7646

ADDITIONAL RESOURCES

Florida High School Athletic Association
www.fhsaa.org
1-352-372-9551

Florida Parent Educations Association
www.fpea.com
1-877-ASK-FPEA

Home School Legal Defense Association
www.hslda.org
1-540-338-5600

Home Education Foundation
Florida Homeschool Lobbyist – Brenda Dickinson
www.flhef.org

FLORIDA STATE UNIVERSITY SYSTEM

Florida Agricultural and Mechanical University
Tallahassee, FL   32307
850-599-3000
www.famu.edu

Florida Atlantic University
777 Glades Road
Boca Raton, FL   33431
561-297-3000
www.fau.edu

Florida Gulf Coast University
10501 FGCU Blvd., South
Ft. Myers, FL   33965
800-590-3428
www.fgcu.edu

Florida International University
11200 SW 8th Street
Miami, FL   33199
305-348-2000
www.fiu.edu

Florida Polytechnic University
One Poly Place
4700 Research Way
Lakeland, FL   33805
863-583-9050
www.floridapolytechnic.org

Florida State University
600 W. College Avenue
Tallahassee, FL   32306
850-644-2525
www.fsu.edu

New College of Florida
5800 Bay Shore Road
Sarasota, FL   34243
941-487-5000
www.ncf.edu

University of Central Florida
4000 Central Florida Blvd.
Orlando, FL   32816
407-823-2000
www.ucf.edu

University of Florida
Gainesville, FL   32611
352-392-3261
www.ufl.edu

University of North Florida
1 UNF Drive
Jacksonville, FL   32224
904-620-1000
www.unf.edu

University of South Florida
4202 E. Fowler Avenue
Tampa, FL   33620
813-974-2011
www.usf.edu

University of West Florida
11000 University Parkway
Pensacola, FL   32514
850-474-2000
www.uwf.edu

INDEX